# SO...
## You're Having a
# TEENAGER

Published in 2020 by Murdoch Books, an imprint of Allen & Unwin

Murdoch Books Australia
83 Alexander Street, Crows Nest NSW 2065
Phone: +61 (0)2 8425 0100
murdochbooks.com.au
info@murdochbooks.com.au

Murdoch Books UK
Ormond House, 26–27 Boswell Street, London WC1N 3JZ
Phone: +44 (0) 20 8785 5995
murdochbooks.co.uk
info@murdochbooks.co.uk

A catalogue record for this
book is available from the
National Library of Australia

A catalogue record for this book is available from the British Library

ISBN  978 1 76052 543 9 Australia
ISBN  978 1 91163 261 0 UK

Cover design by Lisa White
Cover illustration by Cathy Wilcox

Typeset by Midland Typesetters
Printed and bound in Australia by Griffin Press

10 9 8 7 6 5 4 3 2 1

# SO...
## You're Having a
# TEENAGER

### AN A-Z OF
### ADOLESCENCE
#### FROM ARGUMENTATIVE TO ZITS

## SARAH MACDONALD & CATHY WILCOX

murdoch books
Sydney | London

# WHAT TO EXPECT WHEN YOU'RE EXPECTING...

So, you're having a teenager? Congratulations! And, equally, commiserations. When you found out you were having a baby, you were thrilled and everyone was ecstatic for you. You were showered with endless advice, fabulous playsuits and a book boasting a cover with an insipid hippy woman in a rocking chair. Your bundle of baby joy arrived and life transformed. You possibly learnt to purée pumpkin while on a conference call, sing nursery rhymes while preparing a PowerPoint, put on mascara while rocking a pram with your foot. You got good! Your baby survived and bloomed.

Now your baby is gone, transformed into a teen, and no one is cooing or offering to babysit anymore. Once you worried about a drug-free birth, now you worry they are doing drugs. Once you worried about meeting milestones, now you worry they'll meet the wrong crowd. Once you filled albums with photos of cuteness, now if you sneak a shot and post it on your social media you'll be screamed at again – just like when they were six weeks old and arsenic 'hour' lasted from 5pm till midnight.

Kids warp time. The years from babyhood to the end of primary school inch by as if time is climbing a steep and massive mountain. When your baby turns 12 you are at a summit. You look at the beautiful view and your beautiful kid and you are filled with the power of your ascent, the glory of their gorgeousness and the satisfaction of great work. You don't have long to catch your breath. Child-raising descends so rapidly into adulthood that together you career down that mountain in a kamikaze bolt. The path is bumpy, twisted and strewn with obstacles you didn't see coming.

We cannot straighten this path for you and we cannot move the stones that will trip you up. But with this book we can hopefully accompany you during those years that no one talks about beyond foreboding groans. We hope to make you feel less alone, or, at the very least, to make you laugh.

First, full disclosure from us. Sarah was an awful teen. Although, she would like to state for the record that it was not she who graffitied the school changeroom with the C word, but she did deliberately fail home economics as a feminist act, paint her locker purple and yellow, and throw chocolate cake at the Deputy Principal when her out-of-bounds picnic was discovered. Her school report was telling: 'Sarah would rather compose dirty ditties, entertain the class and act the fool than work to her capacity.' At home she was belligerent, grumpy and generally vile. Her mother laughed at Sarah a lot – and no wonder: her crimes against fashion included pointy white ankle boots, multi-coloured ruffle dresses and a haircut that was curly on one side and shaved on the other. And let us never speak of the Madonna phase.

At university Sarah wrote her Psychology thesis on adolescents, but nothing prepared her for having teenagers. Luckily, her teens are nothing like she was.

Cathy was a late bloomer. She was prim and proper, sweet and sensible. She played tennis, was polite to her teachers and did well at school. Her secret rebellion was to draw mocking pictures in the margins of her textbooks and her only sin was being a chatterbox. School reports describe her as 'a pleasant and cheerful member of the class'. Cathy went to Church Youth Group on Sundays until it got rather rowdy. She spent many hours daydreaming about Bernie Taupin, Elton John's songwriting partner – the fantasies involved her in a long white dress picnicking with Bernie on salad sandwiches made with wholemeal bread. Her crimes against fashion included white lace collars, a Country Road skirt and shirt set, a feather cut and a pair of purple velvet overalls with an appliqué apple on the front pocket. Cathy's quietness meant she could be boy crazy and drink cask Moselle without her parents suspecting a thing. She only slightly rebelled after she left school, and then only when it was safe and fully legal. It's safe to say we would've detested each other if we'd ever met as teenagers.

While we understand your anguish about your adolescent, this book is not an attack on teenagers. We genuinely love today's teens – because we will need them to take care of us when we are senile and slobbering. This is not a book of woe or mockery. We consider the teenage years to be far more fun than the toddler years, as these young people become increasingly interesting, fabulously fun and just damn lovely. Sure, they can be surly and snarly. But only to you. Most of them seem delightful to us: incredibly intelligent (are they a genius generation?), freakishly talented, socially conscious, incredibly competent, wise, witty and far better individuals than we were at their age. Look at Greta Thunberg, Malala Yousafzai,

Emma Gonzalez and your own fabulous child. They're rallying for action on climate control, they've grown up with #MeToo, same sex marriage and you . . . a wonderful parent!

Having a teen means you will experience movies, music, books, gigs and life with them in a way that brings endless discovery and you will together occasionally dance to the same 'vintage' music you loved at their age (which they now dig in an ironic way).

But, while they may be wonderful, they are still teenagers. And teens have always been infuriating, bewildering and occasionally frightening. These days they have a lot of extra issues to contend with; they are the iGen or Generation Z – hyper-connected from birth. Early research shows they are conscientious and hard-working, but they're also seen as anxious, fragile worriers who need reassurance . . . and TikTok . . . and Snapchat . . . and Instagram . . . and a better phone. *Now.*

The generation gap has never seemed so small, yet loomed so large. We might like the same music, but the childhood of today's teen has been completely different to ours. Hence our confusion.

This book is to help you with that; to perhaps even assist you in enjoying your teen's journey through puberty and adolescence. It's not a bible; we are not experts. See it as a companion. Dip in when you need a laugh. Turn to it when you've had a door slammed in your face. Have a flick through when you're waiting in your car outside a 'gatho' until you get the text that they're coming out and you must stay in the car and not make eye contact with their friends. Give it to a friend when their child starts high school, performs their first eye roll or begins to smell.

But please hide it from *them*. It's secret parent business.

So, read on. And remember, you've got this. We see you, we hear you, we're with you.

Sarah and Cathy as teenagers

A is for... argumentative

# A

## IS FOR . . .

ARGUMENTATIVE, ATTITUDE,
AGEING, ANGST, ANXIETY,
AWKWARD, APPROVAL

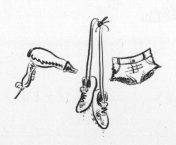

## ARGUMENTATIVE

Perhaps it's because they are trying to separate themselves from you, but the teen can argue endlessly about nothing. If arguing were an Olympic sport, the teenager would be a champion in rigorous training, requiring a carbohydrate-rich diet and constant practice. But only on you. You might suggest that one day they argue as a lawyer, so that they can buy you a holiday house. But they won't, because they will argue against any suggestion you make. In fact, they will argue about anything and everything – how good a song is, the best way to do a science experiment, whether the sky is blue, that up is down. When you begin to bang your head on the steering wheel, they might pause and admit they don't know why they do it.

Sometimes arguing is less infuriating when the arguments are actually *about* something – the house rules, misbehaviour or school subject choices. But, whatever the topic, you need the patience of Job. If you have a teen who likes to argue, *do not*, whatever you do, encourage them to do debating. Therein lies the path to madness. You will be at a constant disadvantage, your arguments breezily dismissed as *ad hominem* and 'straw man'. Although, at the very least, debating kids might play by the rules.

## ATTITUDE

Remember when attitude used to be a good thing? Then that plucky tween grew pubes and 'tude. There's nothing like the rude, withering, grunting salvo of teen to parent, delivered from under a falling fringe or over a cold shoulder.

Attitude can come any time after 12, but seems to peak at 15 years. Requesting that your teen unstack the dishwasher is now akin to asking them to endure an operation without anaesthetic. That child who curled on your lap, grabbed both your cheeks and declared you 'beautiful' now looks at you with eyes that say, 'You are stupid, ugly, irrelevant and awful'. Because now you know nothing and they . . . well, they are the font of all wisdom (or the 'suppository of all wisdom' as an Australian Prime Minister once said, which is oddly fitting as the teen is likely to be talking out of their butt).

The great news is that it reduces the need for Google – your adolescent is now able to frequently correct, hector and lecture you with their strong opinion on everything from art and architecture to zippers and zebras. Your history degree or teaching diploma is now irrelevant and, what's more, zippers are boring and zebras suck. Attitude can come either with lip or in a sour, lemon-sucking snarl. (Although we particularly enjoy the flounce and flicking of ponytail: it's so brutal and yet simultaneously so banal.)

Take heart. This shocking attitude is reserved particularly for you and most likely never seen by others. It's because you know them better than they know themselves. That's petrol on a fire for the teenage brain. You're infuriating.

But *you're* not allowed to be infuriated. The worse their attitude, the more positive, calm and happy your attitude to life needs to be. There's a reason the Dalai Lama and other Buddhist monks don't have kids: it's impossible to maintain equanimity in the face of this barrage of attitude and intense whipping-up of argument.

## AGEING

Teens seem to age fast. They transform overnight. And having a teen spectacularly speeds up your own ageing. Teen years are like dog years: for every year your teen ages, you age seven. To them, you seem old and irrelevant and you might, at times, feel it.

## ANGST

Angst is defined as 'anxiety and frustration that isn't specific'. Teens often feel angsty about the state of the world, or about the state of their homework, or about the state of their toenail polish. Angst is real and it's intense. Imagine living with everything turned up 30 per cent higher in your brain; it's bound to make you dark. This is why the school syllabus favours dystopian novels.

Angst is why some adolescents love the Goth look. They love the edge of darkness – on a sunny day they're 25 per cent Nick Cave, and on a dark day they're full of anguish and angst that only a good Cave song can plunder and purge. Except Nick Cave is an old, weird dude to them; My Chemical Romance is more their jam. Encourage them to express their angst in songs and poetry, or in a diary that you must never read.

## ANXIETY

The teens of today have the highest rates of anxiety of any generation in history. While life in many countries is safer than ever, we live in a time of great change, and many people feel distinctly unsafe and anxious. The teenager even more so. As their body changes and their brain rewires, anxiety flares like a bushfire in a heatwave.

In the US, nearly a third of adolescents aged 13 to 18 will experience an anxiety disorder, with the incidence among girls far outpacing that of boys. In Australia, more than half of all girls suffer an episode of depression or anxiety during their teens. There's evidence that the late teen years are particularly fraught.

Some commentators say that it is parents who are at fault here. It's probably a far more complex interplay of forces than that, but *our* anxiety is possibly contributing to *theirs*. And our anxiety about them being anxious is definitely not helping. Try not to get sucked into their vortex; teach them self-care and problem solving. Don't tell them not to worry: it won't work. Instead, help them discuss and unpack what they worry about. Say things like: 'I can see you're worried about this; I'm here to help. Let's work it out. I know you can do this.' If their anxiety becomes a disorder that is stopping them socialising, or giving them physical symptoms or panic attacks, go to your GP to get help.

We're a bit concerned that anxiety is contagious, especially in high-performing schools. Be aware but not alarmed if you hear of it, and consider how much you overprotect. In *The Coddling of the American Mind*, Greg Lukianoff and Jonathan Haidt write that we need to stop overprotecting our kids. Teens need to seek out challenges, rather than think they are fragile and in danger and everyone is out to get them. This is one of the reasons people move to the suburbs, where kids can climb trees, run riot in local bushland and play on the road. They do. A bit. Until they decide it's more fun to watch other kids climb trees on Netflix.

Your teen will come across other anxious teens and they will catch some anxious thoughts. We're excited about mindfulness and meditation being taught in schools, because if you ever tried to suggest that yourself at home, they'd undoubtedly scream 'boring!' and march off in a huff.

## AWKWARD

They are so awkward, it's awkward to watch. The only time they don't feel awkward is when they're asleep and they are probably having awkward dreams. There is nothing to be done; eventually they will learn to live with the skin they're in without feeling 'totes awkie'. Be aware that lots of things are awkward: weddings, parties, walking, talking, being. Sometimes odd things are awkward . . . We know a teenager who can't go to the local shop if a certain staff member is there. This staff member knows his usual order and that familiarity and intimacy is just so awkward that the teen would rather starve than enter. So much can be awkward, it's impossible to predict. We love watching a group of awkward teens: it's half excruciating and half adorable.

# APPROVAL

Your approval counts. A bit. A tiny bit. What counts more is peer approval. The kids' committee. This is more fraught than a UN committee on human rights.

As a case in point, you will find her a lovely dress for the school formal; she looks glorious even in a changing room under the glare of fluorescent lights with her school socks on. She takes a photo and sends it to a friend, who comes back with a thumbs-up emoji and the words 'So beautiful, I love you'. You will buy the dress. You will get home and she will post it on the group chat and one committee member will say 'No, too formal,' or 'No, blue is not your colour,' and they will all pile on and that dress will be shoved in the bottom of the wardrobe and never seen again. First-world problem, but not good for future credit card approval.

B is for ... body

# B

## IS FOR . . .

BODY, BRAIN, BELONGING,
*BUFFY THE VAMPIRE SLAYER,*
BLACK AND WHITE, BEDROOM,
BATHROOM, B.O., BINGE
WATCHING, BODILY FUNCTIONS,
BOUNDARIES, BULLYING

## BODY

In the teenage years those bodies change from manageable little powerhouses to bumpy, swollen, hairy, oily, leaking, expanding, out-of-control containers with elbows. Early puberty makes teens self-conscious. As does late puberty. As does all puberty. Sometimes it happens so quickly that they are all arms and legs and bruises caused by bumping into doorframes and furniture. One day a friend's son ricocheted out of his bedroom grabbing his neck and screaming 'What the hell is this? Oh my God, I'm dying! It's a lump!' It was his Adam's apple. It had popped up overnight out of nowhere.

Teenagers might stop seeing their body as something that can cartwheel and ride a bike and play cricket and, instead, as something that is imperfect and not good enough. We will talk later about the curse of social media and life editing, but adolescents are constantly looking at images of bodies that have been toned by all-day gym routines, starved by silly diets, sculpted by surgeons, botoxed by beauticians, made-up by make-up artists and filtered by the filtering thingy. All of which makes it impossible for them to wise up and realise how beautiful they are.

Boys are not exempt at all – they endure endless photos of buffed square bodies so muscle-packed that they look like condoms stuffed with walnuts. This means they might suddenly want to go to the gym to pump up those pubescent muscles.

It's important to help teenagers develop a good relationship with their body. Let them celebrate what it can do and the pleasure it can give; how it can catch a wave and ride it to shore, kick a ball, draw a picture, do backflips, ride a skateboard. Show them the way by being kind to your own body – treat it well and be thankful for all it does for you. If it fails you, be gentle with it. Don't model self-hatred by criticising your own body; don't go on mad diets that don't work anyway. Don't constantly comment about other people's bodies in front of your teen and judge people by how they look. Talk about health and fitness and strength, not weight and fat and flab.

# BRAIN

It's not just the teen body that is building itself bigger and better. The teenage brain is under construction. It might seem like it's operating on a yearning for love, coolness, good marks and a desire to snarl and hit out, but it's actually doing much more than that. Knowing what's going on inside the teen head will help you gain more understanding and compassion.

Neuroscience shows the teenage brain is remodelling and rewiring; it's pruning bits it hasn't used, while reshaping and reconnecting. These fundamental changes in brain circuitry are much more powerful than hormones, and they bring great promise and huge vulnerabilities. The brain matures from back to front. The last lobe to develop and integrate is the frontal cortex, which may not be fully functional until a female is in her early twenties and a male reaches his late twenties. This is the part of the brain involved in abstract thought, making decisions, controlling impulses and curtailing pleasure seeking. It is also the part that can conceive of the future and the consequences for stupid actions. The amygdala develops early and the teen brain uses it far more. It's deeper in the brain and it's not rational – it's intense, instinctual, emotional and reactive; it's primed for pleasure and it's not good at seeing the perspective of an old fart parent. That's why your teen might act impulsively, misread cues and emotions and engage in risky behaviour. Their brain is emotionally intense and ready to explore. As teens get older, the centre of brain activity will move away from the cruder response of the amygdala and move towards the frontal cortex.

Teens also have big synapses passing signals around their brains, which means they can learn fast but overload easily. Stress causes overload. Yelling at them causes overload. Imagine a jar full of glitter and water. Shake it. That's a teenage brain when it's upset. Wait until the glitter has settled. Now talk to them.

## BELONGING . . .

. . . is everything. They need to feel they belong in their school, in their friendship group and even in their family (you are a source of sustenance and strength, no matter how unlikely they are to admit it). There are all sorts of groups, just like there always were. There are the dorks and the pretty people, the sci-fi nerds and the sporty types, the VSCO girls and the e-boys, the emos and the lads, the brainy cool kids and the brainy dags, the hippy punks and the punky hipsters. They might need to belong to one group or they might take pride in not being confined, but they need to belong to something.

## BUFFY THE VAMPIRE SLAYER

This 90s classic series is the best thing to watch with a teen girl *ever*. Buffy is the chosen one and she and her dorky friends save the world, a lot. Ok, it might be dated and the special effects are shocking, but it's an allegory of teenagehood that's entertaining with witty dialogue. It can lead to great conversations about losing your virginity, being a nerd (it's a superpower), violence, alcohol, drugs, feeling invisible, rejection, popularity, heartache, death, self-harm, unrequited love, sacrifice, teen pressure ... Plus, it's pre-botox, so none of the actors have lips that look like a swollen baboon bum.

## BLACK AND WHITE

For your teenager, everything is black or white. There's no grey (except on your head and, thanks to your teen, that is probably increasing rapidly). For an adolescent, everyone is an angel or a devil, wonderful or stupid, brilliant or idiotic. This goes back to their teen brain, which polarises everything, just like Twitter, and geez this is hard to deal with when you are older and understand nuance. Their extreme thinking means it's hard for them to be kind sometimes, or compassionate or understanding. Teach them to cut the world some slack and hope the world will do the same for them when they make mistakes.

## BEDROOM

You know you've got a teen when they begin to disappear into their bedroom and shut the door. You know you've got a teen boy when you walk past and catch that unmistakable musty whiff. It's a unique odour that combines dirty washing, wet towel, Lynx deodorant, a mushed banana in the bottom of a schoolbag from

last term, possibly a mouldy mouthguard and a whiff of that other smell that shall not be named. Yes, we know that's sexist, sorry. Some girls' rooms can be just as messy and nearly as smelly. (*See S is for Smell* for tips on getting rid of this.)

Teens have messy bedrooms. It's a fact. So, do you clean it? Do you scream 'CLEAN YOUR BLOODY ROOM' like a banshee on daily repeat? Or do you leave it?

Only you can decide what you can live with; but remember, you don't have to see it – you can always shut the door.

Kids can't Kondo. We know that your teen doesn't always spark joy, but in just the same way that *you* can't de-clutter yourself of them, *they* just can't de-clutter those food wrappers, old t-shirts that don't fit, childhood books of nostalgia and smelly socks and jocks on the floor. Mainly because they just can't see the mess. And if they literally can't see it, then forget it. Under the bed just doesn't exist for them; it may as well be Mars.

You might be paying the mortgage or rent, but for a teenager their bedroom is their sanctuary. It's a life raft in a broiling sea after a shipwreck. It's the only place they can be alone and unwatched. They need to be alone. And, frankly, we need to be away from them. Especially when they arrive home with a face like thunder. Let them shut the door and retreat from the world. Can you blame them? If it's really desperate, you might want to deliver a milkshake to that shut door, knock and run.

So, we let our teens have a messy room as long as it's not a health hazard. If they want to paint it the colours of their footy team, or purple and black, we say, whatever. Well, maybe not black. A bedroom should be private as long as you are not worried about their safety. If you are, go in.

But your teen will also need to come out of their room. We suggest occasionally changing the Wi-Fi password, then they'll spring out like a jack in the box. Or call 'dinner'. Or 'dessert'. As to what you allow in there, well, that's a live debate. A phone they could be on all night? A computer they could be on all night? The girlfriend/boyfriend they could be on all night? It's up to you and depends on their age, but perhaps a door-open policy with some or all of the above is worth considering.

## BATHROOM

We never understood the fashion for new houses to have three bedrooms and five bathrooms. We wondered if these were for people with chronic UTIs or bowel issues. But now we get it. Teenagers need to look in the mirror. A lot. They need to put on make-up, blow-dry hair, gel hair, shave, pop pimples, poop and preen. And they need to just stare at that person they are becoming in awe, wonder and confusion.

Bath bombs are great gifts for teens – those grotty kids who wouldn't bathe now suddenly need a long soak or three long showers every day. This means they will create clouds of steam, lots of mould and possibly drain your hot water system and the national dams. Perhaps they are getting super-clean, or they need the blast of water to wake up, or they are doing something else (*see M is for . . .*). You can scream, pound on the door, turn off the hot water, turn off the water at the mains – or you can get a bigger hot water system and a rainwater tank. Some parents install a ten-minute timer or charge pocket money for each extra shower a day. Teens are generally passionate about climate change so try to talk to them about dam levels and water shortages. Share the bath water. The least grubby goes in first. The grittiest last.

## B.O.

We are baby sniffers. When our babies were young we would sit for hours, playing with their little star-like chubby hands and smelling their beautiful bald heads. Babies and toddlers smell pure, sweet, delicious and divine. Perhaps that's why it's such a shock when they grow up and get body odour. It happens suddenly: one day they walk past and you catch a whiff, or you give them a hug and are hit by the reek of armpit. Your gorgeous baby now stinks to high heaven and you have to break it to them and take them to choose deodorant. It's a moment that might make you cry, but at least your eyes won't be watering from the stench anymore. A basketball court, in particular, can feel like an insulated panic room of teenage body odour.

The deodorant deal is significant and has rules attached. We believe in roll-on deodorant, meaning we have forced our kids into a particular type of social death; but roll-on is much better for the environment than aerosol and doesn't stink out a room so badly that you might actually faint upon walking in. For boys,

Lynx is king in the zoo. While it's particularly odious for adult nasal passages, the boys love it, because . . . irony. It boasts 'notes of watermelon and dark vanilla' and chemical cocktails that only dogs and 14-year-old boys can detect. They seem particularly drawn to the 'African safari' product, because what kid in western suburbia can resist the colonialist appropriation of African sexual power?

The smell is so exotically powerful and intoxicating that it has proved to be life saving. After a 13-year-old English schoolboy fell into a river and was submerged for 25 minutes, he was rushed to hospital and remained in a coma. Staff and family sat at his bedside talking and playing music for three weeks without a sign. Then his mother sprayed his favourite Lynx deodorant. He opened his eyes immediately. That's a powerful force.

Girls may love deodorants with a rather rosier bouquet. Floral and sweet – eye-wateringly so. Sometimes BO is better than the deodorant. Keep the windows down in the car if the chemicals make you sneeze.

## BINGE WATCHING

Sometimes they come out of their room looking like a possum with big eyes. Then you realise you haven't seen them for three days. They've just binge watched six seasons of *Brooklyn Nine-Nine*. Netflix and other streaming services are chill-out zones where they can cut out the world and enter another.

## BODILY FUNCTIONS

If you have a boy you will get farted on. Burps are big too. These will be big, brutal and in your face and they will be frequent. Warn them that when you are old and senile the payback will come.

## BOUNDARIES

It's the perennial question: how tight to set the boundaries? But set them you must. Teens need boundaries for their behaviour, actions, screen time and socialising. You are not their friend: you are a parent. You can't completely trust them and if you don't set limits they won't be able to set them for themselves. Many parents struggle with the boundary issue, but it's your job to set them, not just the responsibility of our schools. It's hard to find the perfect zone, but vital that you do. Boundaries shouldn't be too constrictive – teens need room to grow – but they should be firm enough to give a feeling of safety and security. These limits can be negotiated as they mature and learn to balance privilege and responsibilities. As they grow they will learn to set their own boundaries for behaviour. And won't you be proud?

## BULLYING

You might still have nightmares about the treatment you got at school. But bullying has now evolved to be possibly more subtle, invisible and all-pervasive, thanks to the online world and mobile phones. The fact that your child can be bullied while they seem safe at home in their room and show no physical signs is, quite frankly, terrifying. Bullying is destructive and damaging and teens will feel alone and helpless. They might refuse to go to school, be extra moody and be increasingly isolated. If your child is being bullied in person or online you need to stay calm and listen. Talk to them about teachers and fellow students they *do* trust, be across their social relationships, help them strategise to feel safe, or contact the school to activate their anti-bullying policy. It's not easy to monitor social media and be aware of what is happening, so communication with your often uncommunicative teen is key. Raise them to be smart users. (*See S is for Social Media.*) There are services and helplines for those who need trusted advice.

Perhaps the only thing worse than your child being bullied is finding out that your child *is* the bully. If the school contacts you with such allegations, take it seriously. If you see them behaving badly on social media, call them out.

Try to raise a compassionate child with a good heart who is respectful of difference. We need more of them in the world

C is for ... crises

# IS FOR . . .

CRISES, CRUEL,
COMMUNICATION, CRUSHES,
CLOTHES, CONFIDENCE,
CONSPIRACY THEORIES,
COOL (AND HOT), CONSENT

# CRISES

Teens have constant crises. These can be as banal as leaving their laptop at home or as monumental as does God exist? It is feasible for a teen to have at least three in a day: a PE crisis (lost pants, couldn't skip), an identity crisis (am I still the same person with a different hair cut?) and an existential crisis (you go to school, work, have kids and die; what is the point?). That's a whopper of a day. It is exhausting for the teen; exhausting for the entire family.

The existential crisis is particularly tricky to solve with sweet treats. Teens are starting to think philosophically. This is huge. (If you know the meaning of life then share it with your child and please, write to us via our publisher.) If you believe in God, be prepared for them to question the family faith. If you are a hard-core atheist, they might find a friend in Jesus. It's hard to watch them grapple with the big questions and not be able to provide them with the answers. While everything can feel like a crisis it's also important to stay calm and not catch their catastrophe (*see D is for Drama*).

# CRUEL

Sometimes they are brutal. You come home from the hairdresser and they announce, 'Mum, you look like Mr Spock'. You've suited up for a night out and they declare your outfit 'gross'. You're practising for an important presentation and they murmur casually, as they pass by on their way to the fridge, 'That's cringy' or 'You look old'. Lesson here: do not look for personal validation from your teen.

## COMMUNICATION

This is the most plugged-in teen generation of all time, constantly connected to each other, and to the world. They are connectors, with more Instagram friends than they will ever meet. They can communicate quickly, with pith, banter and brilliance; however, they are shocking at communicating with you. *You* will text into a void and call to a default voicemail greeting. Communication with you is strictly for demanding a lift from the bus stop, asking if they can hang with their friends after school, or to scream:

THE BIOLOGY TEACHER IS MEAN

I HATE HER

If you send a beautifully composed and grammatically correct text and receive a character or two in reply, consider yourself a winner. That na, yup, k (no, yes and ok) are golden gifts as miraculous as picking all seven numbers on Lotto.

However, real communication is vital. Encourage them to tell you stuff, and not just about themselves but about the minutiae of what others are sharing online; you just don't know when it could be useful. But know you can't force them. Good chats will happen spontaneously and when you least expect them: in the car, while walking, while watching TV. These side-by-side conversations are far preferable to the teen than face-to-face inquisitions. While family dinner is a ritual for teenagers to at least observe communication techniques, don't expect in-depth stories about their life. However, when it's late and they're avoiding bed, it's amazing what subjects can come up.

## CRUSHES

The intensity of the crush cannot be underestimated. For your teen, it can feel as if that person they suddenly adore has infected every cell in their body and they are utterly consumed and engrossed. Don't tease them. Don't call it puppy love. Puppies are cute; this is not. It's *everything* and it's *intense*. They are emotional beggars on the streets of love.

Psychologists say crushes last four months – after that it's love. The only time to worry is if their crush becomes an obsession that's starting to interfere with their ability to manage life; less having a Tom Holland screensaver they kiss goodnight and more that they can't eat or sleep and seem soulsick. This may mean they appear unhinged and even creepy to others and even to you, who loves them the most. Try to help them understand that crushes are an ideal without a reality (get them to imagine their crush on the toilet or at least to know their crush might not be all they hope, may be insecure, treat people poorly and, shock horror, not be perfect). Sometimes kids have to pretend they have crushes to go along with the crowd – it can be a performance art. But if it's real, know that the road from feeling they can hardly breathe when they see their love object to 'they are dead to me' can be a very long one.

## CLOTHES

One day that child who would happily dress up as Yellow Wiggle and wear decade-old hand-me-downs will suddenly refuse to get dressed. Congratulations: your teen has found fashion, or 'fashun'. This is all about their self-expression and is deeply influenced by the psychology of needing to belong, as well as a good dose of commercialisation and capitalism. It's also about your excruciation. Shopping with a teen is torture. No matter how hip you think you are, you have simply no idea what they should be wearing and everything you suggest will be 'disgusting'. We guarantee they will only seek out and wear clothes you

hate: the tiny shorts, the huge chunky shoes, the jeans that are more hole than denim. This is the natural order of things. You need to let them try different looks and find their own style, especially if they are paying for it. Remember, in Westfield no one can hear you scream. There is good news though: at some stage, they may discover that the fashion industry is, in the main, wasteful and unethical. Together with this knowledge and their heavy-duty dose of irony, they will find vintage, meaning that the clothes you are still wearing become 'ironic retro'.

Clothes are generally kept anywhere except where you want them to be. On the floor, piled on the bed or on the bathroom sink. Teens can prove they know how to get the laundry in – by bringing in the one item they want to wear and leaving the rest on the washing line as the rain starts.

## CONFIDENCE

We all know those super-confident teens who behave as if they rule the world. But they are a minority, and their parents probably worry they are too cocky.

Self-confidence is the Achilles heel of the teen. They are intensely self-critical and have not perfected the adult instinct to 'fake it till you make it'. A sideways glance from an acquaintance or a bad mark at school can crush their confidence to new lows. When you tell them they're wonderful they may well say, 'Well, you would say that: you're my parent'. But keep saying it anyway. The reason teens are so lacking in confidence is that they feel there's an audience observing and judging their every move. The latest research reveals it's more important for them to practise self-compassion than self-confidence. Try to teach your teen to be kind to themselves. Self-compassion is not about facemasks and self-care; it's about not beating themselves up when they stuff up, and about trying to be better, rather than thinking they are bad.

## CONSPIRACY THEORIES

The world is run by shape-shifting lizard people whose leaders include the Queen, the director of the FBI and Justin Bieber. The earth is flat (believed by a young teen we know who has flown around it), the pyramids were built by aliens, the moon landing was fake and Britney Spears' breakdown was a cover-up for a major American government disaster. Your teen might believe all or none of these, but will probably know about them all. They might also believe in the Mandela Effect and Darth Vader as proof of this; people think he says 'Luke, I am your father', but he actually says 'No, I am your father'. Got it? No? Don't worry, it's teen logic. Our favourite conspiracy theory is that Beyoncé and Jay-Z run the Illuminati. How do teens know this? It's elementary, dear parent – the symbol of their record company is the triangular symbol of the society, Blue Ivy translates to 'the devil's daughter' backwards in Latin, and Beyoncé holds her fingers in 666 circles or as the all-seeing-eye-of-Lucifer when she poses for photos. Convinced? I thought not.

You can argue with the conspiracy-loving teen, but they know that you are wrong and the God-like encyclopedia of proof and the fountain of all knowledge that is YouTube is right. You can quote rigorous scientific study, historical evidence and Einstein – they will quote you a weird-looking American comedian who is posting videos from his parents' basement.

Fake news and misinformation is a huge issue for us all, but our kids can be especially vulnerable. Practise media literacy and critical thinking in your household. Teach yourself, and them, how to be critical consumers and not believe in rubbish.

## COOL (AND HOT)

Being cool is important, but perhaps not as important as it used to be. We live in the age of the geek when it's cool to be a dork. Kind of. But there's cool and there's cool. We don't know the difference because we are adults and, if you think you know, you are kidding yourself. Cool is a cultural cachet with a logic that shifts and is so subtle that only teens sense it – like dogs and those high-pitched whistles. What's tricky is that the more they try to get it, the more it will elude them, because cool involves pretending not to care. Often, though, being cool seems to be about acting older. It can be worrying to watch teens trying to grow up too fast; it might make you want to yell 'Slow down, kid'.

Your teen might never care about being cool, or you might be able to tell them what your own mum probably told you: that the cool kids end up the non-cool adults and that the dorks triumph in the end. This is now backed up by some psychological research done in the US. Researchers have tracked the 'cool' kids and found as young adults they had more difficulties in relationships, were at greater risk of alcohol and drug abuse, and engaged in more criminal behaviour than their 'uncool' peers. While the cool kids seem more grown up, they're often more immature. So, perhaps we need to worry when our teen is cool, rather than if they're not.

'Hotness' is now a social currency that is more important than cool. That does not warm our old cold hearts.

## CONSENT

Please talk to your teen about consent. Show them the cup of tea video as a starting point. It compares initiating sex to asking someone if they'd like a cup of tea. If they say 'I'm not really sure,' don't make them drink it. Don't get angry at them for not wanting tea. If they change their mind when you bring the tea, they are under no obligation to drink. And it's vital not to make someone a cup of tea if they are unconscious. It's an easy, non-embarrassing way to initiate the conversation. Teens need to realise being drunk, horny and flirted with is not an excuse for sex. Just because the fire has been lit shouldn't mean they can't put it out again. There's a lot of careful discussion to be had here about female and male roles.

Make sure your teen knows the age of consent where you live (usually 16 or 17 but younger or older in some countries). Ensure they know the age of the teen they are keen to have sex with.

Tell your teen there are age-difference laws in many states and countries – when they turn 18 they need to be aware of this, so they aren't having sex with someone much younger.

Remind your teen that having sex with an underage girl who's too out of it to give consent is rape.

Remind your teen that making out with an underage girl who's too out of it to give consent is sexual assault.

And that filming a sexual assault on another person is illegal.

And that it is illegal to share any such video unless they are showing it to the police.

Tell your teen it is illegal for them to ask another under 18 for a nude photo and to receive it.

Tell your teen to delete any sexual photo they receive and that if they share graphic photos of other underage teens and revenge porn they are 'trading in child pornography'.

It is hard for teenagers to call out bad behaviour of other teens. This is the role of the Upstander, as opposed to the Bystander, who stands by and does nothing. Encourage your wonderful teen to be that person, no matter how hard this is. Cultural change is slow and difficult, but anecdotally it seems a lot of kids are getting better at telling others their behaviour is not on. Teens are developing their moral compass and in most cases that comes from you, not the school and not their friends. Unfortunately, when alcohol and drugs are involved, issues around consent become more fraught. But knowing the law, having your support and your high expectations will help them develop an understanding of consent.

D is for ... drugs

# D

## IS FOR . . .

DRUGS, DICKS,
DEVICES, DRAMA,
DRIVING AND
DRIVING LESSONS

# DRUGS

During the teenage years we recommend Valium, white wine and, if needed, HRT. We're joking here. And we probably shouldn't. Because Valium is a benzo that is abused, and drug abuse is not funny. We also acknowledge that lot of us make these jokes when we're not coping, to reduce our fear.

Drugs are scary. There's no denying it. Just remember what you used to get up to. Can you even remember?

The good news is that our teenagers are, on the whole, more sensible than we were. Today's adolescents are drinking less – a National Drug and Alcohol Survey in Australia found a whopping 82 per cent of teens don't drink at all until they are over 17. So, while you might have been swigging on Kahlua and milk or rum and coke at their age, thankfully, it's more than likely that your child is not a chip off your old blockhead.

The bad news is that those who *are* drinking aren't drinking bad cask wine like you might have done: they're doing vodka. They can disguise it in water bottles because it's colourless and odourless. They think it's non-fattening and sexy – even when it's smuggled into a party in yoghurt-squeeze containers stuffed in a bra, or dug up out of the daffodil bed (*see P is for Parties*). Other teens are sucking on alcoholic drinks mixed with sugar and caffeine and that's making them both drunk and hyped up.

Most schools have great education programs now that warn about alcohol use, about the dangers of choking on their own vomit, and about always calling an ambulance if a friend collapses. Talk to them about what they know and what they don't know. Be the parent they are not afraid to call if this happens: you might get vomit in your car and you need to be prepared for a lot of responsibility for other people's kids, and a lot of stress and quandaries, but you won't run the risk of them hiding their bad behaviour and getting into worse trouble. Unfortunately, there is a toxic drinking culture in many Western societies – it's difficult for teens to resist and be the boring one who doesn't swig. If they find it hard to counteract the peer pressure, teach them the old bartenders' trick of pretending to sip their drink and act a bit pissed.

If your teen is out and, you suspect, drinking, then you need to stay up and stay sober. And if you supply alcohol to anyone under the age of 18 you can be charged by the police. It is hard to display any moral authority over your teenager when you're in cuffs.

Then there are the other drugs. The sucking of nitrous oxide gas or 'nanging' has resurfaced lately; teens buy canisters of whipped cream, empty the gas into a balloon and suck it for a rapid rush of euphoria and a brief high. Tell them prolonged use can lead to incontinence. Weirdly, amyl nitrate (poppers or 'jungle juice') is also becoming popular in certain groups of teens; once a gay sex drug, this also gives a fast, quick hit. The use of cannabis in teen populations had declined significantly since the 90s, but appears to be on the rise again. If your teen asks if you've ever smoked weed, you could try the Clinton defence – but we advise honesty instead. We admitted to inhaling, but only after waiting until our teen brains had stopped growing, because cannabis can send the teen brain into short circuit. We also stressed that the pot is stronger and possibly more dangerous today – and that it's illegal to use it recreationally in most countries.

It's important to talk to teens about harm, while keeping the communication lines open. The legendary Paul Dillon, founder of Drug and Alcohol Research and Training Australia, strongly suggests discussing drug use in an honest way because scaring the pants off teens risks over-exaggerating the harms, leading to your words being dismissed and ignored. He recommends building an ongoing dialogue and avoiding overly simplistic messages and warnings such as 'just say no' and 'drugs are bad'. Talk about use and misuse, risks and dangers.

There are also synthetic drugs bought online to be aware of today. On top of that, chemical drugs, such as ecstasy, can be laced with all sorts of nasties. The love drug is becoming increasingly popular because it's got a lot cheaper since our day – one pill now costs around the same as two or three coffees. The debate about pill testing at music festivals is about harm minimisation and it isn't the only solution. MDMA makes inhibited teens feel sexy, sexual, beautiful and that the world is wonderful. But it's your job to let them know that pill could be mixed with anything from bathroom cleaner to the horse tranquilliser Ketamine. Police are warning that they've encountered aggressive violent teens who have bought pills they think will make them feel love, only to find them laced with ice. Teens are also trying Valium, Xanax and methamphetamines, which are highly addictive. Again, educate your teen about drugs – if you don't, someone else might.

Give them information, know they might experiment, remind them that anything they swallow, smoke, suck or snort could hurt them. Be alert but not alarmed. Experts state that the later a teen starts using drugs and alcohol, the better for their brain, any future drug-taking habits, and their health. So, delay it as long as you can, using whatever factual and respectful tactics work for you. Some parents in the US now drug-test their teens. This is hard core. It shows a distinct lack of trust – on the other hand, it does provide the teen with an excuse not to partake.

If your child develops a drug problem that is impacting heavily on their life, do get help. Qualified professionals can help you unpack why they are using and if it is related to mental health issues. If you suspect your teen could be dealing drugs to feed their addiction then . . . oh heck, big hug. You need to firmly set boundaries for what is acceptable in your home and that illegal activity is not. Some experts suggest you tell them to stop immediately or you'll call the police, others that you tour a juvenile justice jail to scare them straight. There's a lot of work to do to help them change their behaviour and social group – you may need to take some time off to focus on your teen and get help, including a treatment program.

The good news is that teens are drinking and taking fewer drugs than previous generations. But, while they might be behaving better than you did, they have a different, pressing problem. All those times you wore your undies on your head or argued with your friends or behaved like a jerk at a party have been consigned to history. But today's teens have mobile phones recording their messiest moments. Their pickled brain can't appreciate that one day they might want to be an MP, or a teacher, or a doctor and that photo might get in the way – at best, as an embarrassment, at worst, losing them the job. You could give them a 'wipe your digital profile clean' gift for their 21st birthday. Don't panic about it though: it seems increasingly likely that any Prime Minister of 2040 will have a massive, coloured-sleeve tattoo and a racy Tinder or Grindr profile lurking in their past. But none of that means you shouldn't keep trying to warn them.

# DICKS

Teenage boys adore their dicks. All of a sudden, this tiny little thing becomes swollen with possibility and thrill. This means they must keep their phone away from it. What's more, dicks and balls are infinitely hilarious. Your young boy could find it hard to resist his desire to draw dicks on dusty windscreens or his school books. This penis passion shall pass when they grow up and get to use it instead of worshipping it. Make them clean the car as penance. And, once again, keep that phone away from it.

# DEVICES *(also see P is for Phone and T is for Technology skills)*

Yes, they are devoted; some say addicted. Whatever they are, so are you. If you've resorted to putting your hand over their Instagram feed while they are favouriting pouty classmates, or have threatened to throw their laptop out the window, or have hidden their iPad under your pillow, you are not alone.

Historically, every generation of the human race has grown taller than the one before – perhaps until now . . . could this be the first shrinking generation, due to their permanent slouch from tilting over a screen? These digital natives may, if you're lucky, understand that they can put down their devices and look up; they just don't want to. The phone *(see P)* is like a third hand for them, but for families it's a huge source of tension, distraction and infuriation. You can try the 'devices basket' at the front door, the locking up of screens at 7pm, have long conversations or bark orders about internet use, or push them outside for a walk, patting them down before they leave to check they aren't carrying. We've tried them all. Good luck. We do recommend occasionally getting off your own devices to show them it can be done. Hypocrisy is a great luxury you cannot afford.

## DRAMA

We love drama as a school subject, but many teens love it as a lifestyle choice. For some teenage girls, there is only one volume: an exasperated, infuriated scream that is LOUD AND DRAMATIC.

You probably can't fix the drama – especially if it's about relationships with other teens. The best thing to do is to listen calmly and help them find a solution, using phrases such as: 'What have you done that's helped before in this situation?' Or at least acknowledge quietly that their world is small and their feelings large; they can bounce off that enclosed world and reverberate. Perspective comes with calm chats, age and experience. For those days when *everything* is a drama we suggest you help them channel it by trying out for the school play.

There are empathetic parents, who pick up on their teen's drama and catch it faster than a cold on a plane – their heart beats faster, their breathing turns shallow and suddenly they're yelling back, 'I *KNOW* THE GEOGRAPHY TEACHER IS AN IDIOT'. If this is you, we empathise. We suggest headphones or imagining you are in a bubble of light so that the drama cannot reach you.

## DRIVING

Congratulations. Having a teenager means you now also have an unpaid job as an untrained chauffeur. Those growing legs can't cope with walking – you need to pick them up from the bus stop, take them to soccer, or to netball, or to drama, drop them off at guitar class and then fill up the car with the petroleum you're ruining their world with. We prefer teenagers without too many hobbies, or at least ones they can travel to straight from school. And if you are picking them up in the evening, do keep your day clothes on: turning up at their friend's house in your chenille robe and Ugg boots is generally frowned upon.

Use this time together. Driving is a good chance to engage in conversation – you can look at the road while you talk to them about sex, drugs and rock and roll. They're trapped: they don't want to walk, so they must indulge you. Driving them everywhere is a pain in the butt, but nowhere near as painful as when they want to take the wheel.

## DRIVING LESSONS

Step one to approaching driving lessons with your teen is to ask your partner or someone else to do it. Step two: ask them again. Step three: take 10 deep breaths, in through your nose and out through your mouth. Imagine you are a yogi on a mountain in Tibet and you are floating. Nothing can touch you and that wheel that just mounted the roundabout at speed is but a grain of sand on a beach. Don't flinch; don't white-knuckle the door; this too shall pass.

Actually, learning to drive does not seem to be the rite of passage it once was. Many city teens don't seem that excited about it, making do with public transport and Uber; although many still see it as a ticket to freedom. In Australia, teens now need about one zillion hours of driving practice documented in a logbook before they can take their driving test. The most popular method for achieving this seems to be to start driving around a cemetery (everyone is already dead) or, when they are better, a family road trip to the Australian Outback (or to the sea if you already live in the Outback) with the teen driving. You will move slower than an antique collector's caravan and find it more stressful than a performance review with your new-and-much-younger-than-you boss, but it will all be worth it. Advise all relatives to give money for driving lessons for birthdays and Christmas – and a day-long defensive driving course is worth bucketloads of logbook hours.

When your child passes their test and is licensed to drive unsupervised, remind them about the responsibilities of the road, their probation period, and requirements and rules. Also talk to them about accidents. We know teens who got into a crash and had no idea what to do. Let them know they must get the other driver's licence number, and the phone numbers of any witnesses. They need to wait around for police, if they've been called, and for an assessor to check if the car is safe to drive and a tow truck if it's not. The lovely teens we knew did most of this correctly and then drove off so they weren't late for their movie. In a written-off car.

E is for...embarrassing

# IS FOR . . .

EMBARRASSING,
EYE ROLL, EYE CONTACT,
EGOCENTRISM, EVERYONE
ELSE, EXAMS, ENTITLED,
EXTREMELY EMOTIONAL,
EXPECTATIONS, EVERYTHING
SUX, ENTERPRISING,
EATING DISORDERS

# EMBARRASSING

You are. Yes, you. You are *so* embarrassing. Don't walk beside your teen; walk ahead or behind them. If you are anywhere near them, walk quietly. More quietly than that. For God's sake, your shoes are too loud on the school stairs. Everyone is looking at us. Don't chat to any person on the street. Stop it. Shut up. You can't wear that outfit: it's too tight/short/daggy/try-hard/colourful/boring/young/stupid. Do you have to breathe so loud? Just stop breathing altogether. Oh, for God's sake, stop turning blue; you look stupid. You're so embarrassing.

Never try to be cool in front of your teen. Or funny. Do not *ever* dance in front of them. Don't talk to their friends. Don't take photos with them.

Of course, we do all these things. Some parents just love making their teen cringe and set out to do it daily. If that's you, enjoy. But, really, isn't it just too easy? Like shooting fish in a barrel.

# EYE ROLL

Ah, the eye roll. Behold the magnificence, the talent, the artful perfectly timed execution ... You'd imagine this to be a skill requiring genetic predisposition, high-intensity training and constant practice. And yet, this ubiquitous eyebrow flounce seems to appear spontaneously during early teenagehood and then disappear a few years later, leaving no trace.

Biologists point out that, due to the level of whiteness in the human eye compared to other primates, we have been given a particularly remarkable ability to communicate using eye movement alone. Parents of teens point out that we tend to use that ability to the maximum during an intense three-year period. It could be that eye-rolling is a passive or immature sign of aggression, intended to demean the other person in the conversation. Or it could be that they know you're the boss and hate you for it.

It has been suggested that an eye roll from an adolescent girl establishes that she is an 'independent state electing to yield, for now, to the regional power'.

Whatever it means, it's as uncontrollable as a fart. And, for your additional pleasure, it can also be delivered with a withering dose of side eye.

## EYE CONTACT

Lack of this is the one thing that might make you miss the eye roll. After years of training them as toddlers to look people in the eye, your teen is now likely to start hiding behind their fringed-curtain hairstyle or finding a certain spot on the floor transfixing. Some people blame technology, but it's quite possible that cave-kids in the middle of puberty also couldn't look their elders in the eye. It's a side effect of their lack of self-confidence and their withering sense of feeling constantly on display and judged. You can try the 'look at me, look at me' chant, or you can gently encourage their eyes to fleetingly travel upwards and know it will probably pass. And, if you see another teen in the street and they look you in the eye and possibly even speak to you, then grab your phone and report this wonderful interaction immediately to their parents. That mum or dad will be so pathetically grateful they might cry with joy. At the very least they will be skipping on air.

## EGOCENTRISM

This is their developmental stage. It means everything is all about them. Other people are just props in their performance. They are the Sun – you and the rest of the family are just space junk orbiting around them. Nothing matters but their pain and their feelings; nobody else could possibly understand, nor feel the same. This egocentrism might seem selfish and self-loving, but it actually corresponds to low self-esteem. This means that as egocentrism reduces, teens feel better about themselves. They know they are selfish: you actually don't need to rub it in.

One day they will see you as a person, not just a parent. They'll see the driving around you do and the food you make them, and they'll appreciate how hard you work to keep them in Wi-Fi. But don't hold your breath.

## EVERYONE ELSE . . .

'. . . is allowed to get their ears/nose/eyebrow pierced, drink, go out all night, stay at their girlfriend's/boyfriend's, have their phone in their room all night, play Fortnite until 3am, so why can't I?'

Eye-roll them.

## EXAMS

We have a school system that is based on constant assessment and tests – to some extent your teen has to suck it up and live with it. Exam period is a time for chocolate, walks around the block, special treats, their favourite dinners, tip-toeing around the house and painting them a pot of gold at the end of that inverted rainbow of fifty shades of crap. Some teens can study at home alone, others need companionship and stimulation of a study group, some prefer a library. This will change as they age. Groups become fun in the last years of school, as they can support each other and revel in their shared pain. But do let them know that they are more than just a final mark and that there are many paths in life. (*See G is for Graduation* and *U is for University*.) Don't expect executive planning for exams. Do expect last-minute panics.

## ENTITLED

If your teen wants a Gucci wallet for their thirteenth birthday, we acknowledge that entitlement could be an issue. We know a teen who has been flown first-class around the world and another who refused to go to school camp because it was 'too gross'. If you have an entitled teen, you could blame the extreme capitalist society in which they live, but you might need to take a look at your attitude as well.

The vast number of teens live non-privileged lives. Help them out by arguing for educational and social policies that help *all* teens, not just your own. Over-entitlement can be a weakness, and often those kids who've had to build resilience end up more mature than the overly precious sweeties. And even those who are somewhat entitled are often aware of the problems in the world, and that they are being saddled with climate change, debt, changing job markets, uncertainty and division. They are entitled to a future that we haven't stuffed up for them. So, to quote a teen here, 'check your privilege'.

## EXTREMELY EMOTIONAL

This is so obviously the teenage state that it almost goes without mentioning. And yet, it's everything when you are tiptoeing around it, plunged in the depths of it and terrified by how low the lows can be. Imagine feeling so flayed you are almost without skin? That's how life often feels for a teen; they are too raw, too naked for this world in so many ways. It's their brain – that underdeveloped limbic system we talked about in *B is for Brain*. That amygdala is flooded with hormones and so disconnected from the rational brain command centre that it renders them raw and reactive. They can wake up in the morning in tears that could be about physical exhaustion, emotional overload or mental messiness, or all three at once. They may not even know why they are in floods of tears, or they might think they're upset because someone hurt themselves in the basketball game yesterday and once they start crying everything else floods in and they just can't stop. These raw unbridled emotional extremes are also caused by the tsunami of hormones washing around their body. Add in a dose of society pressure, exhaustion and a sometimes brutal education system that isn't a good fit for everyone, and you get emotional collapse. When you pick up a teary teen, try to listen to their pain. Make them tea in bed, rub their back, scratch their head and give them a huge hug. Extreme emotions can also be scary. If your teen feels totally out of control or doesn't come out of strong feelings for a long time, do take extra special care of them and consider help. Sometimes *you* need help to help them.

# EXPECTATIONS

We all want our teen to do well at school, in sport and in life. We see the parents of tweens timing their child's 50 metres butterfly at the swimming carnival, hiring a pro to perfect their tennis swing, and spending the weekend filming dance eisteddfods. We've heard parents on the sidelines of cross country carnivals promising their child a new iPhone if they win. Then, when those same kids are in the thick of adolescence, the same parents may realise it's time to adjust their expectations.

We've overheard many a parent re-evaluating from 'I expect all As and the School Cup in Athletics' to 'If they stay alive and out of jail, I'll consider them a success'. And we concur. It can be a brutal comedown from wanting your kid to be a doctor to wanting them to survive high school, but it's important to adjust your expectations to the situation in which you live. You can be anything from a mouse dad to a tiger mum to a practitioner of benign neglect. It's completely up to you, but some kids go so far off the rails that life becomes about keeping them safe and yourself together. Strength and love to you if you're in that situation. It's good to have standards but it's important to keep an eye on the impact of your expectations and whether they are lifting or hurting your teen. We should all have expectations about our teen's behaviour, decency and humanity, rather than their performance.

# EVERYTHING SUX

At times, it can. Let them write it on their arm and then wash that temporary tattoo away in a soothing bath. Remind them ice cream doesn't suck. Or chocolate. Or seeing some live music. Or watching a movie with popcorn. Help them to find things to alleviate those days and look forward to something – however small that might be.

## ENTERPRISING

We know a lot of very enterprising adolescents. Some are trading in white goods, designing graphics for websites, creating T-shirts or selling baked goods. Encourage and reward this and please can they meet our kids and pass some of it on? Unless they're selling drugs, then see *D is for Drugs*.

## EATING DISORDERS

Many teens feel uncomfortable with their bodies, but sometimes this dissatisfaction can become a mental health condition. Families play a huge role here. Try to model and create a focus on good health, rather than talking endlessly about your own body or others' physiques. And don't go on and on about dieting. Teens are getting enough damaging information from society about weight and worth: home should be a healthy retreat (not a health retreat).

An eating disorder is first and foremost a mental health condition. Disorders include anorexia, bulimia, binge-eating disorder and now some new types. Orthorexia is an eating disorder that involves an excessive preoccupation with eating healthy food – but there's nothing healthy about it. And now some boys are at risk of 'bigorexia', or muscle dysmorphia, when young men become locked into a desperation to bulk up their bulk with more bulk.

These conditions can cause long-term physical and mental harm and incredible distress to their families.

Look out for excessive dieting or overeating, excessive exercise, a teen avoiding parties and dinners or social situations that involve food, a child exercising obsessively and talking a lot about body image and food. If your teen loses a lot of weight, always wears baggy clothes and disappears into the bathroom after dinner, then be alert. There are some good online checklists that can help you decide whether to be alarmed. The sooner you talk to your teenager and get them help, the better. In Australia the Butterfly Foundation is a great place to start and they can give help for the entire family.

F is for... fault, and failure.

# IS FOR . . .

FAULT, FAILURE,
FORMAL, FREAKING OUT,
FOOD, FRIENDS, FAKE TAN,
FAKE I.D., FANTASIES

## FAULT

It's all yours. Everything. Deal with it. Their weird feet, their too curly/straight/thin/thick hair, their inability to do calculus, their fear of spiders . . . You did it to them. Shame on you.

## FAILURE

They will fail and that's ok. Mostly, it will be your fault (*see above*). And that's ok too.

## FORMAL

This can be a source of much excitement and/or excruciating stress. And, oh, the palaver. For some fifteen- and sixteen-year-olds, the school formal or prom is the most important night of their lives. Hopefully, by their final year of school, they've calmed down enough to actually enjoy themselves. The source of stress usually centres around who they will take and what they will wear.

If your teen does not have a love interest and has shown little interest in one, this can be tricky. Suggest they don't take anyone, especially if their friends also aren't taking dates – they'll save money, not have to look after someone they used to play tag with in primary school, and have a good night dancing with their friends. Or they could just take a plus one, a friend of either sex. This tactic requires a friendship group with a similar attitude. If they're part of a social group that thinks boyfriends/girlfriends are the most important thing in the world and you have to have one on your arm, things can be harder. Co-ed schools obviously have the advantage here – plenty of options among classmates.

If your teen has a boyfriend/girlfriend of the same gender, the formal could be fraught or fabulous. Especially if they have not yet come out. (It must be said that the entire 'coming out' thing is totally old school for many kids, who quite rightly point out that no one feels compelled to 'come out' as heterosexual.) But some schools still ban same-sex formal partners. Your teen must navigate his or her school culture here and if they want to challenge it they will need a lot of support from you, including a warning that coming out at a formal is quite possibly not the best way to do it. There are some wonderful videos and photos of surprise formal dates being presented to families and friends – but there are also probably many (not saved to YouTube) that didn't work out so well.

Regardless of who they take, know that it's not your job to find them a date. Suggesting the boy/girl down the road or your bestie's teen, who's despised them since playgroup days, is usually not helpful. Also, remind your teen that keenly inviting a girlfriend/ boyfriend seven months in advance and then breaking up with them can create a super-angsty situation. Negotiating this can be akin to the Korean peace settlement.

You might have worn a shot taffeta dress with a drop waist or a hired tux with a light-up bow tie to your own formal, but your teen cannot. Girls often want a drop-dead glamorous dress that costs the equivalent of your weekly income. If you pay up, like the sucker you are, be prepared for them to say it can't possibly be worn on a second outing. Try suggesting they swap with friends of the same size, or hire a dress – better for the environment and the bank balance.

*The most important thing* for the teen girl is that her dress must not be the same as anyone else's on the night. If this happens it will be a horror show that will 'ruin her life' (*see D is for Drama*). Luckily, there will probably be an Instagram account set up eight months before the formal where teens stake their claim to a certain dress. Some girls get their outfit sorted that far in advance. Really. Others buy three dresses and return the two they don't want. This is not fake news. These teens will talk about the formal every day for months; some will want matching shoes, professional make-up, a spray tan, hair extensions, bikini waxes (best not to ask), fake nails and a blow dry. They'll want to do all that stuff in the afternoon in their 'girl gang' so they, apparently, need to book months ahead to beat the pack. If you have a teen like this, you have our sympathy, but not our credit card pin. And a rookie warning: do not let them get the spray tan on the day of the event if they are wearing a white dress (*see F is for Fake tan*).

Most boys want a suit (linen for some populations, hipster suede for others) and perhaps sneakers. They might have to buy a corsage for their date. Prepare to be surprised by how much a withered flower on a ribbon band can set you back.

And for those kids who want to hire a stretch hummer limo, we say, WTF? But hey, you might think that's fab and, there's no doubt, they'll think you are fab if you stretch to paying for it. It's all about the fun photos, after all, and these must also be organised well in advance, especially in regards to who they appear in the photos with. You might be ok with all this or, like us, resolutely lo-fi on the whole formal business – perhaps you have a teen who is happy with a cheap outfit, a cool pants suit they got at a thrift shop, pale skin and hair and make-up done at home. You are lucky; perhaps you can even go out to dinner before you pick them up. Your teen could always pay for it themselves if they want 'the look'.

But beware, how they look is only one aspect of the evening. Today, there are also the vitally important 'pres' (before party) and 'afters' when some kids will have alcohol. (*See P is for Parties*.) If you elect to host, choose the 'pres' every time. You will need to provide a good backdrop for photos, some carbs on plates to line their stomachs, snack food that doesn't drop grease on dresses, paper straws so they don't mess up their lipstick and perhaps some fake champagne if they are that way inclined. You are brave and we salute you and we hope you spied on them from the kitchen. Don't they look gorgeous?

## FREAKING OUT

It could be a spider in the bathroom, a funny–blasé comment from a friend, the fact they don't know anyone in their class, a knock-back after an audition ... all are disasters that could lead to a freak-out. A freak-out is a blowout. It can clear the pipes and the mind. Maybe we should just allow one a week. 'Is this your Friday freak-out? Good, go for it, I'm listening.'

## FOOD

When boys are having a growth spurt, things can be fast and furious in the food department. We're not recommending bar fridges, due to climate change and electricity costs, but you might consider hiring one when your son turns 14, or upgrading your

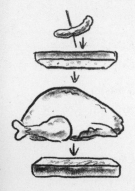

fridge to giant size. Or don't bother, because no matter how well stocked your giant fridge is, he will swing it open 10 times a day and groan 'There's never any food in this house'. Teenage boys can need a pie at 4pm, a toasty at 4.30pm, a chicken at 5pm, a cow at 6pm and will still yell 'What's for dinner?' from their room at 6.30pm. After dinner they need a loaf of bread, a milkshake and an orchard of fruit with some ice cream. Then they will wake up the next morning 10cm taller. This massive growing and chowing down may stop suddenly at around 18, and then they'll become vegan to impress the gorgeous healthy-eating girl in their class. Teach them to make their own snacks or you'll never get anything done at home.

We talked about Eating Disorders (*see E is for . . .*) but know that a lot of teens can become obsessed with food these days. Food must not only be good for you now, but it must also look pretty and photogenic. You must plate up well at home and old favourites like spag bol will be met with a moan because it's ugly as well as boring. Watch out for young Instagram 'influencers' who eat nothing but 59 bananas a day, fast frequently or only eat organic wholefoods grown by chanting monks in Bhutan. Some foodie types may be harmless, but some can be barmy and dangerous. Teens need to eat properly for health and energy. Food should not be a full-time job.

# FRIENDS

By age 15 the teen's friends seem more invaluable than you are. What their friends say in a casual aside can undo three months of careful conversation you've been cultivating. Friends are enormously important – and it's enormously important for you to find out who they are. Ask your teen about their mates. Generally, kids are attracted to like-minded others – but not always. And, while all your child's friends might be 'good kids', the group dynamic can bring out the worst in all of them. Including your angel.

The entire Princess Bitchface/Prince Boofhead thesis seems rather harsh and simplistic, but there is often a dominant and destructive force in any group. If your child is the leader, try to help them realise how their power can be destructive. If they are at the mercy of other kids and in a toxic group dynamic, it can be deeply upsetting. Ringing the parent of their problem friend is often not useful. Help them work things out themselves, rather than ordering them to 'stay away from that child: he/she is revolting'. Perhaps tell stories about how your friends are supportive and loving, and model being a good mate. Try asking 'What have you done in the past when you've had friendship issues that might help now?' Workshop some solutions and behaviours they can adopt. Then go into your room and stick pins in the doll that looks like your child's tormentor.

By the last couple of years of school, the friendship stresses tend to calm down.

## FAKE TAN

It is always fun to pass time at the netball court by comparing shades of fake tan on display. Some days the opposing teams can look like Donald Trumps with ponytails playing stretched Oompa Loompas. Watch out in particular for the fake-tan line that ends at the neck, so that the face is pale and the body bright orange. We realise they consider pale skin horribly ugly, but if your teen is going down this route, perhaps help with application and warn about overuse – and good luck getting it out of their white umpiring uniform.

## FAKE I.D.

When we were young we'd head off to music gigs with our fake IDs and spend the entire car ride memorising the fake name, fake birthdate, fake signature and fake star sign as an extra safety measure. These days licenses have photos but teens can still buy fake IDs from friends and websites, or make their own using Photoshop and technological skills that are light years ahead of yours. Fake driving licences or university ID cards or other forms of fake identification are used to buy alcohol and get into pubs and nightclubs. You have to make your own decision about how concerned you are about this (we have heard of a parent who bought one for their child as a birthday present). In some states it is a crime to use a fake ID, so keep an eye out for it in their wallet.

## FANTASIES

Chances are your teen has a rich inner life you don't know about. Teen fantasies can be elaborate and detailed and wonderful but they can also be weird. Try to remember yours and be understanding if your child reveals their dreams. We'd like to single out JK Rowling for criticism here. Yes, she's incredible and, yes, she got millions of teens reading and, yes, we absolutely love her books and her charitable donations, but she's also responsible for many kids not settling in to high school because they are waiting for the owl to arrive from Hogwarts summoning them to study in a Scottish castle. For many of us this means ultimately disappointing our offspring, or selling both our kidneys. Thanks, Joanne. Thanks a lot.

Let them know it's ok to fantasise about other teens, social media stars, actors and their own future fame ... but help ground them to earth by reminding them we can't all fly like Harry friggin' Potter.

G is for ... grumpy

# IS FOR . . .

GRUMPY, GUSHING,
GORGEOUS, GATHOS,
GLANDULAR FEVER,
GOOGLE, GAMING,
GRADUATION

## GRUMPY

They are not grumpy all the time. When you don't see them they're usually fine. At school they are, most likely, delightful, chatty, sweet and lovely. At sport, activities and weekends away with other families, butter wouldn't melt. It's just after being non-grumpy all day in those situations they've *had enough*. When they are at home a release valve pops in their brain and that massive wave of grumpiness that's been building bursts over the wall of social niceties and dumps on you. Believe it or not, it's a compliment. It's hard keeping it together all day; letting their grump flag fly shows just how safe and loved they feel with you.

## GUSHING

You get the grumpy and the grunt but their friends get the gush. Gosh, these teens love each other. The boys call each other 'legends' and the girls run out of superlatives as they gush on the 'gram. One will post a photo and they all rush in to comment . . .

omg u r soooo booful I luv you so much

u r the cutest babes eva (plus row of love heart emojis)

luv u 4 eva (plus a pulsing pink heart)

I luv u more (five hearts and a kiss)

I want to crush u w my love

This can crescendo into an intense love fest so gushy and emoji filled that it's like diving into a vat of pink treacly fairy floss. Hopefully, it's all part of the intensity of their love for each other; however, we suspect that at times the gush could be a performance art to stay in the cool crew and on the inside they could actually be dry retching. Hopefully not.

But if *you* send them a love heart emoji, don't expect a return message. There's no gush for you. Indeed, if they are at a party and message you a love heart or gushing text, get in the car and get over there pronto. Or send an ambulance.

## GORGEOUS

They have no idea how gorgeous they are. Sure, there are the really unattractive years where the hair is lank, their skin is terrible, their bodies are out of proportion, their posture appalling, the braces brutal and their fashion frightful. But on either side of those years and, even during them, they are just gorgeous in body, mind and spirit. They are divine creatures.

## GATHOS

Gathos are short for gatherings. They are bigger than a hangout but much smaller than a party. They will know everyone there, it will be cas (casual) and hopefully it won't be advertised on social media and crashed by hundreds of teens they don't know.

Usually gathos are safer than a huge party, but don't assume this means there's no grog or drugs. Parents might be there, but you need to check. And if you are picking up from a party (*see P is for Party*) or gatho we reckon you need to get out of the car, check out the scene and meet the parents who are hosting. You will learn a lot about your teen's social group and you will show them some manners to emulate.

# GLANDULAR FEVER

Americans call it 'mono', Australians call it 'the kissing disease', everyone calls it 'oh no!'. Most adults have the virus that causes glandular fever and chances are your teen has been exposed to it and showed no symptoms or sickness. If so, you are lucky, because some teens will get the virus at a certain age (most often between 15 and 25) and go down like a ton of bricks. One minute they are on cloud nine having had their first pash, then a few weeks later they have massively swollen glands that look like a goitre, temporary liver damage and they are too tired to do anything but lie in bed listlessly looking at their computer. The exhaustion can last for weeks and possibly even months, which is usually way longer than the grand love affair that caused it. There's no treatment except to let them rest, recuperate and hope it doesn't lead to long-term fatigue. Drop sporting activities, ease back on everything and know that they've learnt an important lesson: love hurts.

So if your teen is even more grumpy, listless and grunty than usual, don't tell them to sit up straight and stop being a slob – take them to the doctor for a check.

# GOOGLE

You might be able to remember encyclopaedias; you might even have one propping open that dicky door in your laundry. But to a teenager a book with information is like a Flintstone's car. Google has the answer to everything.

As the parent of a teenager, you will find yourselves in endless arguments about what Google dredges up. You will quote scientific studies that are peer reviewed and used as policy basis for the World Health Organization, but if they read something on Google it's the God-given truth. Google will tell them how to write an essay, how to play bass and the themes of Hamlet, but it also puts them a click away from hard-core porn and total bull. (*See X is for X-rated.*)

## GAMING

Yes, a lot of them love it. It's their down-time, fun-time, me-time and fight-time. Keep an eye on what they are playing and who they are playing it with if they are online. Ask questions like 'Are you sure that other kid is 14, like you?' 'What kind of messages is he or she sending you?' 'Is that character with the giant boobs a strong resourceful female character or a victim?' In fact, why don't you just stand between the teen and the screen and ask lots and lots of questions? They love that.

We've all heard the stories of gamers in some countries who were so addicted they played until they died of dehydration. This is incredibly unlikely to happen to your child. But gaming can be addictive, so seek help if you're worried about it and set some limits and reasons for why it comes after homework.

You could also pick up the control console and understand what they're doing and why. Be curious about their passions and you might realise they've learnt some skills without your help. Sometimes you need to enter their world to understand it. (Although, chances are, you'll just go hoarse from yelling 'Turn it off'.)

## GRADUATION

At the end of school this happens. What a moment. It will mean so much and signal that the end of teenagehood is nigh. If you pay school fees you'll suddenly be wealthier, but it might hurt your heart.

Not all of them come back for the graduation day at school, but those that do often seem graduated in life. They're often tanned and sun kissed, their hair stringy and bleached, their nose pierced or their shoulder sporting a tacky tattoo; their uniforms look shorter, they look exhilarated, a bit wasted and suddenly so much older.

After graduation, all those years at one school with the same people are finished and they're thrust out in the world whether they're ready for it or not. And whether you are ready for it or not. It's exciting and terrifying in equal measure. That safety rug is gone but so are the early wake-ups, the constant testing, the studying, the grading, the rigid rules imposed by the school, the definition of self that a school can provide. The liberation is almost too big, the choices too vast, the plunge too sudden. Option overload is a lucky problem to have, but it can also be overwhelming. Did you know what you wanted to do at 17 or 18, just out of school? You can tell them to go with their interests and what they're good at, but what if they're not sure? Guide, don't push. Hear them, don't hassle. Gap years are wonderful for discovering what is out there and what they don't want to do (*see U is for University*). So, sing that stupid school song with them and celebrate the end of horrible exams and the pain of letting go of friends forged in the fire of high school. Send them off into life with a smile and a sharp pain in your big, swollen, hurting heart.

H is for ... hormones

# H

## IS FOR . . .

HORMONES, HIGH SCHOOL,
HATE YOU, HEART,
HANGRY, HUMOUR,
HAIR, HEARING

# HORMONES

We are all more than our hormones. But sometimes it feels as if they are everything. Tell your teen how oestrogen levels can make them feel terrible grumpiness or despair before their period. Explain that testosterone can make them reckless and horny (*see R is for Risk-taking*) but it can also flare into fury. But let them know their hormones will settle and come under control. And that they are more than just their hormones. Hormones get blamed for too much; they are not an excuse for bad behaviour.

# HIGH SCHOOL

Some parents worry a lot about which high school to send their child to, while most don't have a choice and go local. Parents analyse schools for their results, attitudes, cohort, reputation, 'values', uniforms and much more. Just remember what's important to you might not be for your child and that the school will not define their entire existence. Hopefully your local school is good and welcoming but there will be good and bad days, months and years. If all turns to crap, it is sometimes possible to change schools and this can release some teens from a destructive pattern of behaviour or inescapably difficult friendship group. You won't be nearly as involved in high school as you probably were at primary school, but the more you are the more you will know.

No matter which school your teen attends, it can seem like a big scary zoo that your child enters as a tiny, cute, meek meerkat and leaves as a magnificent lion or, perhaps, a gawky giraffe. Here's our very rough guide to the high school years.

## YEAR 7

They start sweetly, with their huge, shiny, proper schoolbag, their pristine uniform and their deep desire to please both you and their teachers. That first day is both terrifying and exciting for them, and heart-swelling and heart-busting for you. The lump in your throat might throw you flat on your face. Perhaps it's as nerve wracking as the first day of school, but you can't hold their hand going in, cry when you say goodbye, and volunteer for reading groups to keep an eye on them. You must walk away and wait until the end of the day to hear how much the big kids swear and how they got lost and how the canteen is so wonderfully unhealthy compared to primary school.

Within a few weeks of starting high school, expect your child to be overwhelmed with the workload and the emotional overload of changing of classrooms, getting to know different teachers, making new friends and finding their way around. After, hopefully, close friendships in primary school and finishing their at the top of the social heap, they are now often friendless, alone and a small minnow. They might feel lost and confused, or throw themselves into so many activities so quickly that they get overtired and lose it. Question whether they need to do choir, footie, theatre sports *and* environment club and know if they choose too much it's likely they will crash. Within weeks your child could be lying on the bed crying, 'I'll never make any friends; no one notices I'm alive'. Be thankful if yours adapts instantly and is openly thrilled with themselves. It's a big year and a huge transition.

Combine all that with what is probably their first experience of a smartphone, a school laptop, and none of the support that primary schools give and you can get into a tricky too-much-tech-too-soon situation. Some kids who don't know anyone can develop a screen habit as a safety net in a lonely playground. Keep an eye on your baby this year, but don't baby them too much.

## YEAR 8

Just when they've got the hang of high school, made friends and are feeling confident, they might be split up into new classes and feel they have to start again. Year 8 is also the year they begin to feel on top of things and less like babies, so work is often less important than getting an A in socialising or in starting to act up and act out. Some teachers mark this as the year teens can become slightly demonic. We don't believe in hell and think that sounds extreme, but then we don't have to deal with them en masse. This year will see the flowering of the deep desire to want to impress and be accepted by their peers. Lots of girls can get distraught over friendship bust-ups, being dropped as a BFF and other sudden tribe shifts. Teens can get mean or confused while trying to manage their relationships and they might stop telling you every detail about what's going on. That's good in a way (because it can be dull hearing about Zac's spit ball in Science and the purple laces Evie put in her school shoes) but it also means you lose touch with who is who and what's going on. They might lie awake at night worrying about impending world war or a war that's split their friendship group and it's only then at 2am that you hear all about it. The group dynamics can become cruel and more physically aggressive. Puberty divides kids into some who look almost adult and others who are still tiny.

## YEAR 9

It is a truth universally acknowledged that this is a shocking year. In recognition of this, some schools practically give up on academic learning and focus on practical life skills – kind of admirable, as all teens should learn how to iron their own shirt and make you a latte. There is much going on in terms of their social standing and the school group dynamics can look a touch *Lord of the Flies*. Your teen can become rude and disrespectful and too cool for school. This is often the year they are choosing electives and then hate their choice and regret it and spend a lot of time trying to get out of it.

## YEAR 10

Friendships become more supportive and mature. Hopefully your teenager will find their peeps, start calming down and focusing on schoolwork. They will need to choose subjects for the last years of school and this can prove hard for some. How do they know what they want to do, when they still don't know who they are? Are they sporty? Are they into maths and science? Are they arty? What if they are all or none of those things? Tell your teen the decisions they make will not dictate their life. Just because they choose chemistry and physics doesn't mean they can't go to art college or be a plumber. Then beg them to become a plumber – they cost a fortune and always seem to have too much work to come and fix the screaming pipes in our bathroom.

## YEAR 11

This often starts with a brutal shock at the wave of work heading towards them. Around this time many teens are becoming real humans and better company; they could chat to you without criticising your driving, your clothes and how you walk. Or they might be able to do this with other adults, just not you, and that's almost enough. There's a lot going on in their work and social life. There might be a part-time job, parties, partners and a lot of assignments, so time-management is key. So is the self-control to get off YouTube and focus. Some schools hit teens hard now to get them match-fit for final school-leaving exams.

## FINAL YEAR OF SCHOOL

This is the most stressful year of their life to date. Parents hold their breath until the torture chamber of standardised testing racks them up, measures them and brutalises their brains. Your job is to be support crew and coach, so try not to start a new full-on job this year or to be away a lot. They are likely to need their favourite food and your presence; the good news is it will be for a relatively short space of time. The bad news is this will be in retrospect.

Hopefully, your teen will burst from the exam season as a wonderful, gorgeous adult, ready to take on the world. Good luck with that.

# HATE YOU

They will. But that's ok. Love and hate are closer than love and like. They will yell 'I hate you' because you don't let them go out,

you won't pay for their AirPods, you
make them come to family dinner
with the uncle who chews loudly, you
ring the parent of a friend of theirs,
you bust them doing something awful,
and possibly even just because you
know them.

As they try to get to know themselves, nothing is so awful as someone
else knowing them intimately and
profoundly. You made them – that
cellular connection and the fact that you once changed their nappies
and can almost guess the feelings they can't even identify, absolutely
infuriates them. So when they yell, 'I hate you,' yell back, 'Well, I love
you'. Because you do and it matters – even if you don't like them
right now.

## HEART

Your heart is scarred. It's old and it has big bumps from where it
broke and mended, shattered and came back together. Your teen's
heart hasn't done that yet. Their heart is big, beautiful, swollen,
sweet, precious and so very vulnerable. Their first love and loss will
be beyond all pain to them. Their heartache for the person they love,
who hasn't even noticed they are even alive, will leave them reeling.
Try to remember this. Hearts are precious and you don't want them
to be so scarred that they are scared of love in the future. And be
aware that they might not tell you if they *are* heartsick. Look out for

signs of moping, sighing, sadness and even more vague staring off into the distance. You could have a lovesick teen.

# HANGRY

Hangry is when a teen is so hungry they are messy and upset and angry. Give them food. *Now.*

# HUMOUR

Humour will get you through the teen years. Don't laugh at them, but do laugh behind their back. And do laugh with them. When your boy is down and troubled and he needs some loving care and nothing, oh nothing, is going right, do not, we repeat *do not*, sing Carole King to him. It's sexist and gendered to say it, but there's no doubt scatological humour can perk some boys up instantly. Talk about poo and wee and farts, and your hunched-over, gloom-faced son could look up, unfurl and beam like a flower opening to the sun.

Find things that make your teens laugh and share those with them, even if it is Chris Lilley or a bad meme or some YouTube comedian who you feel is clearly a loser. Sharing a funny podcast or TV show can lift spirits.

Humour can become rudely offensive in the mid-teen years and if you express shock they will say 'You just don't get it'. For them it might be about pushing boundaries and group dynamics but you can push back and set limits in your house about how offensive it gets.

# HAIR

Hair must be touched, played with, inspected, split, sculpted, braided, curled, straightened, dyed many colours, and commented upon. It will get shorter as high school progresses for many girls, and longer for many boys, and it can be a battleground for school rules. Head lice can make the leap into high school with them; if the teen doesn't have to wear their hair up for school then lice can persevere. Comb through conditioner every weekend to be safe. Sure, it's time-consuming, but it makes them sit still long enough to do some homework or watch a worthwhile TV documentary. Tell them that if they don't comply, the scissors will come out and a bowl cut will emerge.

Haircuts are a source of tension. And a source of hilarity. The mullet is back, the curtains are fading out; although that could have flipped by the time you've read this sentence. The boys use a lot of product so theirs stands up as if it's in permanent shock, and the girls are often so good at blow-drying they will put your hairdresser to shame.

Facial hair sprouts any time from 13. The bum-fluff on the upper lip is a look like no other. No boy seems ready for it, all appear baffled by it, and most ignore it until you say something or they are teased for having a 'paedo mo'. Dads need to decide when it's time to teach them to shave and enjoy this special moment, while mothers stand outside the bathroom having a wee weep. This can be a hard one for single or two mothers – you could bring in an uncle, a significant male, or teach them yourself – after all, you've been shaving legs and other bits for years. Hopefully, they'll feel all manly and excited rather than crushingly self-conscious. Stay matter-of-fact and positive.

Eyebrows are very important to many girls these days. Eyelash extensions can be stuck on, making them look like they have an eye full of spider legs.

Body hair can be a battleground. Many girls will want to start shaving their legs in high school and you have to teach them so they don't cut themselves. It's a ritual of growing up and you might want to resist, but it's probably better than them being teased? However, fashions change, as we know, and in some circles body hair is definitely making a comeback – after all, it's always been the ultimate display of confidence. Remember the world-startling underarms of Patti Smith, Julia Roberts and Madonna? . . . Not that your teens would have the foggiest about who they are. But it does show why permanent hair removal from some body parts is never a great idea.

You might get asked about pubic-hair waxing and you'll need to make your own decisions about that – perhaps tell them to beware of boys who want them to look like little girls?

## HEARING

Kids are completely deaf to these phrases: 'How was your day?'; 'DINNER!'; 'Please will you empty the dishwasher'; 'Clean your room'; 'Take out the recycling'. They just can't hear them.

Yet, if you are five rooms away and whisper into your phone that you think your teen might have a boyfriend, or that they are going through a tough time, they will come barrelling down those stairs to scream at you. They are like bats. Their hearing can be supersonic.

And there's the issue of earphones and headphones. These appear as permanent attachments from about year 8 and don't come out until teenagehood is ended. Try to persuade them to take them out when they do homework. Many teens swear they must have them in at all times or their brains will fall out. If you pull the plug they will deflate in front of your eyes. If you can't get them out, talk to your teen about turning the volume low so they don't do permanent noise-induced damage; this is on the rise and can be irreversible. Warn them about the dangers of wearing them on skateboards, on bikes and in traffic.

One of us is deaf in one ear from dancing on speaker stacks to loud 80s music. So we should know.

I is for ... independence

# I

## IS FOR . . .

INDEPENDENCE, IRONY,
INTROSPECTION, IDENTITY,
IDEALISTIC, INFLUENCERS,
IDENTIFYING EMOTIONS,
INFORMATION OVERLOAD

## INDEPENDENCE

Your aim here is to do yourself out of a job – when this teen time is over you want them to be independent. We once heard a caller on the radio discussing how he and his wife didn't go to sleep until they had checked on their daughter using a tracking app. She was 28. That's some rather co-dependent parents right there.

We know your teen is your baby and always will be and that you worry about them. But they need to be able to function without you. They need to be able to drive, cook a decent pasta dish, shop, manage a budget, have a relationship and hold down a job. Help them get there. Encourage paid work: if they can't find it in a terrible teen job market then suggest volunteer work; encourage independent travel and interests. Otherwise you will be old and infirm and still cooking them dippy eggs and toast when they are 50.

## IRONY

They are so ironic. But, unlike Alanis Morissette, they know what it is. Everything is ironic and there are so many layers of irony that you won't be able to keep up. Their clothes are ironic, music is ironic, life is ironic. So, jumping into conversations that teens are having must be done with extreme caution. What might sound like sacrilege might just be irony. They are *Reality Bites* on irony steroids.

## INTROSPECTION

Teens might seem constantly engrossed in memes and TikTok, but they are actually introspective and deep. They are often thinking, a lot. Except when they should be thinking a lot. This means they can veer from a burping competition to deep contemplation in an instant. An instant so small that you will most definitely miss it. This also means that any small slight on their character can lead to a deep funk or fresh round of self-hatred. You are living on a roller coaster that veers from silliness to a Sartre-like focus on 'why do I exist?'. They are self-focused and introspective because that's their right, no matter how wrong it might seem.

## IDENTITY

They're finding it. They're experimenting. They're forming. They're trying it on, seeing how it looks in the mirror, adding extra layers, throwing it off and putting it on lay-by for later. Remember all the identities you tried on for size? They will know all the myriad of modern identities and can help you never confuse your VSCO girl with your e-boy. Just don't ever tell them an identity is a phase. Even though it probably is.

They need to move outside their identity in the family. Feedback from peers becomes more important than feedback from you. Kids from a distinct cultural background might feel strength and power in their cultural identity or, if they've experienced racism, they might reject it. This can be hurtful for you as a parent, but it's likely that, with help and support, they will draw on the strength of that cultural identity and come back to it one day. Third-culture kids have to walk a tricky path; they have a unique cultural identity but can feel constantly on the outside, and this can be painful.

But, while your teen will be influenced by friends, school and society, don't forget they're also influenced by you. Values are important. And we don't mean the values of a nice tie or 'leadership' or that stuff you are sold with the school fees. We mean the integrity and decency that you show and that will rub off on them. Although probably not when you are watching and can crow about it.

Society, we hope, is reducing its rigidity and this generation seems more accepting of different identities and diversity. And yet, for a generation that's meant not to like labels, they sure like labels. Teens might identify as gay, bi, fluid, queer, asexual and even straight. A friend's son reported that 'a kid came out as omnisexual today'. When she asked, 'What's that?', her son furrowed his beautiful brow and said, 'I'm not sure. I think he's sexually attracted to everything'. Of course he is: the kid is 14. At that age, saucepans are sexy. Or is that pansexual?

It's great that they are increasingly supportive of preferred sexual preference, but it's also fair to tell them they don't have to identify as anything until they're ready. It's also ok not to know; they can identify as 'a-not-sure-yet-sexual'. Identity offers a calm harbour in a sea of turmoil, a retreat from questioning and confusion – but let them know they are still cooking. (*See Q is for Queer.*)

As they move away from you in the mid-teen years they might become very political and strident in their opinions. You might have a little pain in the butt at the dinner table declaring the way you cooked the corn culturally inappropriate. Admire their passion.

Be slightly detached and yet supportive of their identity shifts. Unless they try on being a cruel, violent bully. Don't support that.

# IDEALISTIC

That idealism we just mentioned is wonderful. See it as a sign of hope. Long may it last. Help them find a cause to champion. Society will try to smash it out of them soon enough.

# INFLUENCERS

Once kids wanted to be firefighters and police officers, astronauts and zookeepers when they grew up. Now they want to be social media influencers. These are people who pretend to be authentic while spruiking make-up, t-shirts, holidays, food, health products and a lifestyle of the rich, famous and fatuous. It's DIY advertising. They might be gorgeous and helpful and inspirational, or they might be ridiculous or revolting and, sometimes, a bad influence.

Find out which influencers your child is influenced by and, if necessary, try to undermine them. If it's a paleo–neolithic–eating girl, refuse to make bone broth soup and remind them that evolution has moved beyond our cave-dwelling days. If it's a gorgeous six-packed boy peddling water bottles that contain life-enhancing crystals, remind them tap water is free and great for the planet. But good luck. Remember, *you* actually are the biggest influencer in their life, they just don't know it yet.

# IDENTIFYING EMOTIONS

Sometimes their emotional intensity is a swirling vortex of different feelings. Helping them work out what they are feeling can be tricky, but important. They need to identify if they are feeling fury, sadness, shame, guilt, love, anger, or any of the other myriad feelings a teen

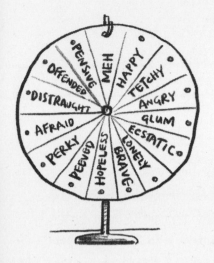

experiences. This will help them express themself usefully and equip them for emotional maturity. Explain to your teen that it is possible to feel more than one emotion at once – in fact, the emotion they're displaying (often anger!) is the one on top, masking the others below that they're not dealing with, such as frustration, rejection and confusion.

If you try to help, don't tell them what they are feeling; rather, suggest what might be going on – this will help them to work out an emotional vocabulary. It can be confronting and might require chocolate for them and a glass of something for yourself. Emotional Intelligence (EQ) is important, becoming more widely recognised and prized, and will stand them in good stead for life.

## INFORMATION OVERLOAD

You have it, they have it, we all have it. Infobesity is on the rise. Not enough quality information is getting through our teens' skulls, because there's too much to take in. Take them out to the desert or the bush or just into the garden sometimes. Have some information-free nights. Wash their brains clear. Give them a brain enema that makes them mind-blowingly bored. Get them to sit around a fire and look into the flames, look up at the stars, or meditate on a candle. They will grumble like hell, but they'll feel better for it later.

J is for... judgement

# J

## IS FOR . . .

JUDGEMENT,
JUDGEMENTAL,
JUSTICE, JOBS

## JUDGEMENT

Their judgement is impaired. As we learnt in *B is for Brain*, the teen brain isn't yet fully cooked. Their prefrontal cortex is like a radio with a fraying wire that crackles in and out of connection. This increases their chances of judgement impairment. To you it's a no-brainer (we hope) that you don't drink until you vomit, or give your heart to a player, or pose for, or send, saucy photos. But logic isn't always perfect for teens. They make decisions that are decidedly dodgy, rudely reactive and bizarre. But remember, this is how they learn and grow and help that brain improve.

A lot of us trust that our teen is the sensible one in the group – and perhaps they are. But don't assume they'll always be sensible. Teens need to be given enough freedom to make mistakes, but not so much that they don't develop judgement.

Try to help them make judgements when they are not time-stressed or upset. If their brain is hot, their judgement is often impaired. If they are calm, they'll be able to access their logical rational side. Sometimes they can't make a decision about anything: their brain is so fried they freeze. Choose your battles. If they can't make a call about what colour undies to wear, tell them to go commando. Try to help them delay decisions if they are all het up. Encourage them to reflect on those decisions, regardless of whether they were right or wrong. Do workshop and work through some possible scenarios with them and help them prepare for tricky situations – and try to anticipate flaws in your plan. For instance, one teen we know had a plan for escaping situations when others were drinking and she didn't feel comfortable. But she hadn't anticipated that the friend she was staying with one night would want to stay at the party and drink. So, play 'let's pretend' with possible scenarios for drunkenness, drugs and disasters. But you can't anticipate everything. Remind them that you are there for them and can take a call, and that if they call you in a bad situation you won't be too . . .

## JUDGEMENTAL

Because, God knows, *they* are.

They are intensely judgy. And that extreme passionate thinking means everything they say can sound like an insult hurled at you as a poisoned dart sticking out of a massive Thor-like hammer. They are judging you harshly, but only because they feel judged themselves. We have a theory that the

most perfectionist, most insecure teens are the most judgemental of all. They are just like adults like that.

## JUSTICE

Teens are definitely attuned to injustice. They have an antenna for being badly done by. They will keenly feel that a certain teacher ignores them, that the school beauty gets all the attention, that the sucker-up gets made tennis captain. It enrages them that life is unfair.

They might not be able to see that they are winning in the game of life . . . they got you as a parent, didn't they? (Good luck using that line – we can see the eye roll from here.) The cruel fact is that they actually need to get used to life being unfair. Because – spoiler alert – it is. (*See U is for Unfair.*) That doesn't mean they can't work to make it more just in the future.

## JOBS

Paid teenage work has changed a lot since we had Saturday jobs on the cigarettes and records counter at Woolies.

While the jobs market for teens is not fabulous, there is still some casual work for 15-year-olds in retail and fast food, which will give them maturity and important life skills such as a desire to never eat burgers again.

Some teens manage to neatly squeeze work into their super-charged schedules, while others feel they can't possibly fit it in alongside study, socialising and learning to drive. There are schools that now insist on volunteer work, which is great but does push paid work into the 'later' basket. Some teens have no choice about working and this gives them great practice with time- and money-management. Beware of endless rounds of trial workdays that never lead to payment.

If your teen wants to be able to afford a car, fancy clothes or a hectic social life then they should take on some sort of work. You can suggest them to your friends for dog-walking, babysitting and odd jobs around the neighbourhood. If you have a kid who plays music, Christmas busking is lucrative (but if you suggest taking an agent's cut to pay off their lessons, prepare for a rockstar hissy fit).

Then there are the jobs teens should be doing around the house.

Some parents insist that chores be linked to pocket money, while we reckon they should be part of family life. Sure, they'll complain that it's boring putting out the bins or vacuuming. Do they think you find it intellectually enriching? Explain that *even you* aren't that boring yet.

Get them to clean their own room, but be aware that if you ask them to do the entire house you might have to reassess your definition of 'clean'. A paint-chipping hurtle down the hall with a vacuum, a greasy cloth smeared over the kitchen table and a throwing of clothes under the sofa cushions might not be your idea of pristine. Some families ask their teen to cook dinner once a week; some will plate up delicious restaurant-quality grub; others make such offensive slop or such a mess that they are never asked again – as was no doubt their intention.

I said I didn't want to post my bum cleavage on Insta and now Jacinta says I'll never be empowered as a woman.

K is for ... Kardashian feminism.

# K

## IS FOR . . .

KARDASHIAN FEMINISM,
KARMA, KISSING,
KNOWLEDGE

# KARDASHIAN FEMINISM

This is a contentious entry, but it's a trend we've noticed because we are middle-aged frightbats. The young women of today are fabulous feminists. Most of them know that women still don't have equal rights in terms of bodily autonomy, safety, wages and career prospects. It's great they know their rights, and many are very aware of discrimination and equality. It's fantastic that they strive to be strong and fierce.

At the same time, they are growing up in a hyper-consumerist culture that has turned feminism into another product you can love-heart on Instagram and buy on a $60 T-shirt. Your mum might have burnt her bra, but your daughter considers it her feminist right to 'free the nipple'. Young feminists are 'body positive' and, while that sounds lovely, when it combines with consumerism (and doesn't it always?) that can lead to a generation gap we're calling 'Kardashian feminism'.

Kardashian feminism means you will hear arguments such as 'I need these fake nails and $80 foundation because it's my right as a woman to look how I want and your judgement is sexist and old-fashioned feminism'. Or, 'You have to let me post frequent bikini shots because it's my body and you are being paternalistic and slut-shaming me'. What looks like commodification of the female flesh to you is empowerment to her. What seems like dressing for the male gaze to her grandma is her notion of 'bodily autonomy'.

Girls mature faster than boys and this sometimes leaves the boys feeling baffled about expectations. We've heard of relationships when girls demand chocolates on weekly anniversaries, a ring after a month of dating and a bracelet at three months. Hopefully, that's rare – because money can't buy you love, babe – and, besides, that level of expense isn't easy for a young boy or girl who's dropping leaflets for real estate agents for $5 an hour. The boys get confused that girls are rating hot guys in undies on Instagram, but if they did something similar they'd get burnt. (This is, of course, probably far less common than boys' sexist behaviour and rating girls, but it's an interesting development.)

At the other extreme, teen boys are watching YouTube videos made by young Incels – angry creeps and sexist cretins who tell other young men that feminists want to kill them, that society hates men and that they need to hate women back.

Sexual politics is a minefield for teens. Adults struggle with it, so, of course, they will too.

Encourage your daughter's feminism into effective solutions towards equality. Encourage your boys to behave with decency. Talk to boys and girls about objectification, sexualisation, sexism, shaming and their behaviour. They might be getting information at school that is helpful but can also be confusing. Watch your own behaviour and how you talk about women and men and sexual politics. Explain to them what the #MeToo movement actually is, not what they might have been told it is.

## KARMA

Consider your teenager as payback for the crap you put your parents through. In the months after you held your baby for the first time, you quite probably looked at your own parents with new eyes.

You realised the sacrifices they had made, the intense love they had for you, the everything they'd done, and your shame was deep . . . almost teen embarrassment all over again.

If your parents are gracious, they won't enjoy this period in your life too openly. However, many grandparents relish the teen years as a payback that fills them with glee. If you say a single word to them about your teen – if you complain, bemoan, whine or reveal – they will turn pink with delight at the chance to remind you of your own hideousness at that age. Even those with ailing memories suddenly sharpen up to zero in on an incident when you lied and got busted for smoking in the dunnies. Their instant razor-sharp recall will cut you like a knife. You can't blame them: you put them through hell and now they can sit back and relish you being put through the same ringer. Luckily, they can only tease about the stuff they know – and that won't be everything. Chances are, *you* got away with a lot more than your teen can get away with in these days of helicopter parenting and constant surveillance.

## KISSING

Remember the thrill of your first kiss? Those gorgeous teenage lips are made for it. Your teen is probably simultaneously yearning and

scared sockless about it. It's a massive moment in their life and, chances are, you won't even know when it happens.

If they ask you about kissing will you tell them to practise on an orange, like you did? Braces can make things awkward and slow down the onset of kissing marathons. But kissing will always find a way.

If you are braver than us, talk to them about saliva and not drowning the object of their affection in waves of spit. And, if exams are just around the corner, remind them it might not be best to kiss the super-cool pale and listless teen lolling in the corner; the one who is actually languishing exhausted and contagious, awaiting the results of their glandular fever blood test.

If your teenager comes home with a pash rash or lovebite (yes, they are still a thing), dig out the skin ointment and sit down for the sex talk (see *S is for sex*).

## KNOWLEDGE . . .

. . . is power. Get to know about their life without prying, by inviting their friends over and meeting their friends' parents. We know this is difficult and makes you a dag, but it's good to know who is who in the zoo. Know the issues at school, who the cool kids are and what's the T (gossip and drama).

As for *their* knowledge, well, they know everything, don't they? (*See G is for Google.*) Feel for them: it's hard to live amongst mere mortals when you have the wisdom of a god. Mind you, they actually *do* know a lot and are wise in rather wonderful ways. They know that reality TV is a falsity, they know that society and world governments have failed to act to secure their future, and they know that social media is a minefield. They just might not know how to act upon such knowledge.

L is for ... lying

# L

## IS FOR

LYING, LAZY AND LETHARGIC,
LOSING THINGS, LIKE,
LABELS, LETTING GO,
LANGUAGE

# LYING

They will lie. Often. But they weren't lying: they were just 'protecting you from information you couldn't digest'. Genius. In a teen head this makes perfect sense.

You might think you know when your teen is lying, but you could be very wrong. The duplicity some teens can achieve is breathtaking. On the surface they seem lovely, content and ambitious – but they can be living a double life. They are smarter than you in many ways: they can hack your computer, forge your signature and impersonate you on the phone. Be aware if you have a child capable of this. Try to channel these talents elsewhere. This duplicity is a valuable life skill in a world in which fake people triumph – they will go far but might do damage later. Demand honesty, but don't always expect it.

# LAZY AND LETHARGIC

Your darling can seem so listless and lethargic and lazy. You can shake them awake, pull them out of bed and then watch them barely able to drag themself to the fridge, open it and stare listlessly. They will lie in bed for hours, twitching only the arm that operates their phone or computer. Sometimes they are so lethargic they just can't form words. When one friend said to her son 'Just answer my bloody question,' he sighed deeply and slumped and, out of the corner of his mouth, mumbled: 'Mum, I will use words, but then you will use words, then I have to use more words, then there are more words. And my mouth just can't do it today.' Life is brutally hard when you have to open your mouth for more than food.

It comes from all the growing they are doing and all the exhaustion of puberty. Or it can come from not enough sleep (*see Z is for Zzzzzz*). But let's face it, most teens are not allowed to be lazy for long. You hassle them too much.

## LOSING THINGS

It's not laziness that makes them leave their PE bag on the train, their phone on the bus and their brain on their bed. It's just that they are thinking about bigger things. Like PewDiePie's latest video and whether Ellie will kiss them one day and whether Sophie meant to blank them in the canteen queue or whether their breath smells. They will get lost and lose things for years. Buy second hand. Label everything.

## LIKE

At times this feels like their every second word. 'So, like, I went to the shops, like, and, like, Charlotte said, like, I love your dress, like, and I said, like, you are so cute, like, and she said, no, like, you are.'

Along with 'so', 'I mean' and 'OMG', 'like' is the 'um' of their era.

Give your teens a topic and ask them to talk for a minute without saying 'um' or 'like' or 'I mean'. It's fun to watch them struggle. Or count out loud every time they say 'like' or 'um'.

I mean, like, I like you and I, like, don't mean to be, like, mean to you...

Some see the humour, yours may not (*see E is for Eye roll*). You need to reduce the 'likes' because they're catching and you'll find yourself at work, saying to your boss: 'I mean, like, um, I really think I, like, need a pay rise, 'cos, like, really, um, I'm unreal.'

Then there are the 'likes' that measure their worth to society. The likes on Instagram and social media. Just a couple of likes is social death to them. That's like walking down the street naked. Likes are a currency that measures belonging and acceptance through a rather awful filter. As social media experiments with not publicly displaying the number of likes on a post, this currency will change and evolve. Likes are vanity metrics; likes don't value their decency and goodness as a person, their behaviour in friendship, their values and hard work. Instead, they measure something that's nebulous and a slave to fashion. Even the teen you consider to have a strong sense of self can be hungry for likes, even though intellectually they know they shouldn't. Talk to them about this. They are so much more than their likes. Ultimately, they should aim to like themselves, but sadly many of them just want to be 'famous'.

## LABELS

For a generation that doesn't like being defined, they love labelling themselves and each other (*see I is for Identity*). The labels around personality can come before they even know what they are. It's all part of identity forming, but let them know that if they are emo in year 8 they can become techno-hippy in year 9 and that if they are a thrash-metal-head in year 10 they can still like indie pop in year 12.

# LETTING GO

You have to do it. Slowly, carefully and steadily. They're going to be adults someday soon and they need to know that the thread to you is strong and powerful (and invisible), but they need to be able to function without you always being there. This should happen slowly and naturally with school camps, adventures and excursions. But don't let them roam the streets at midnight or they'll be able to do all the things you did and worse. Know where they are and who they are with and how they are getting home. Until they are 18 – then they don't have to tell you nothing!

# LANGUAGE

They have their own language (*see V is for Vernacular* for a translation). But this generation also has a full adult language for things they don't really understand. This means they diagnose and label each other with ease and often: 'She's so OCD'; 'He's definitely depressed'; 'Jamie is a sociopath'. They also overuse certain words inappropriately. You might ask where they are and they'll reply, 'Stop stalking me'. You request they clean their room and get accused of 'triggering' them. If you give them a cuddle, they'll say casually 'Get off me, paedo'. This is not appropriate. Tell them so. They'll tell you to 'stop hassling cos it's only a joke'.

M is for ... mumble

# M

## IS FOR . . .

MUMBLE, MONOSYLLABIC,
MOODINESS, MELTDOWNS,
MEMES, MASTURBATION,
MARKS, MONEY, MIRROR,
MENTAL ILLNESS

## MUMBLE

Something happens when the teen hits a particular phase of puberty. Especially the boy teen. All the muscles in his face suddenly lose their tautness. They flop and cave in and he can't open his mouth properly except to utter incoherent mumblings and fumblings. If this coincides neatly with your own middle-aged hearing deterioration, the mumble is a nightmare that can lead to major misunderstandings. But there's no point getting a hearing aid yet – his words will one day reappear like green shoots after a bushfire.

## MONOSYLLABIC

'Hey, Sweetie . . .'

'sup?'

'How was your day?'

'k'

'And how was sport?'

'sucked'

'Did you get into the talent quest?'

'na'

'Are you hungry? Would you like a sandwich?'

'yup'

'Are you trying to kill me with your lack of verbosity?'

'whaeva'

Ten minutes later you walk past their room and they are chatting animatedly, using complete sentences, on a group Insta chat that goes on for hours despite the fact they spent all day with the group. They'll come out and be back to monosyllabic for dinner, which they'll leave to play an online game, where you'll overhear informed, educated and thoughtful conversation about corpse count. Look: words! Everywhere!

You might have laughed, a decade ago, when people told you your child would one day cease his or her constant babbling and bantering and become a monosyllabic grunter. You're probably not laughing now. At around age 14, the babbling brook of stories, singing, commentary and wonderful words dried up. You will regret all those times you asked them to stop talking, and begin to treasure each utterance like a golden jewel.

## MOODINESS

The sighing, the kicking, the grunting, the swearing under the breath. And that's just you.

It feels hypocritical to even mention moodiness. Let's face it, middle-aged parents can be quite moody ourselves. Tell your kids to have their own kids young, because menopausal mothers blended with pubescent teens makes for one moody household. However, at least if these life stages collide you will understand how they feel. Your hot flush might correspond with their cold shoulder, but at least you have the option of HRT.

The amazing thing about teen moodiness is that they can be happy and joyful one minute and dark and stormy the next. A shutter comes down out of nowhere, slamming out the sun. The tears just come and they haven't even had a chance to work out why. So what chance do you have? We like to hug if we are allowed close, or to massage heads and necks and suggest chocolate pancakes or great teriyaki. If the swings get too high and too low for too long consider help. (*See M is for Mental Illness.*)

## MELTDOWNS

It's the terrible twos all over again but with swear words that would make a union leader blush. At some stage of their adolescence you might find yourself living with an emotional terrorist who has the power to plunge the entire family into huge misery or raging fury.

TODAY'S FORECAST

Some sunny periods in the morning followed by an inexplicable meltdown, with storms clearing in time for dinner...

They should not have this much power, but at times they do. If the universe is kind and your child was a terrible toddler, then perhaps they will be an OK teen. They owe you, right? If your toddler caused your hair to drop out, remind them of this karmic deal, frequently.

But all kids have meltdowns. It could be over too many assignments due at once, losing a game, because you hid their x-box controller (you know this is child abuse, right?) or because they have no clue what just happened. We know one teen who said: 'I can't help it. I just feel so weird and angry and I want to just scream and punch things.' Great insights. The smart parents got this teen a punching bag.

## MEMES . . .

. . . are their jam. They are quick, fun things that go up on social media, dominate all humour for a week, and then die. Throwing your woe was one where teens filmed themselves bundling their upset into a ball and then lobbing, kicking or pretend throwing it at someone to catch and contain. It's over now. There will have been some zillion memes since then. They're about group membership and commonality of humour and you are not meant to know about them. If you start re-enacting a meme it will instantly die and it will be your fault; so, please, for the love of Keanu, don't try. Memes are rarely that funny, nor witty; in fact, for we old people they are most often obvious, meaningless, puerile or just plain pathetic. They are worse than dad jokes. But teens think they are brilliant. That's the generation gap right there – we're not meant to get them.

## MASTURBATION

They will do it. It's private and you don't want to know. Let alone have the awkward conversation. But, if there are incriminating-looking tissues lying around their room, suggest that *they pick them up* and if they leave incriminating evidence such as cardboard toilet-roll tubes (yes, that's a thing) on their floor, make sure they clean their own room. If your teen suddenly goes from only washing once or twice a week to having three overly long showers a day, then be aware that any complaints you make about water shortages could be highly embarrassing or go unheard. We quietly suggest you might need to have a dirtier mind about them getting clean and get a solar hot-water tank. We know this is confronting stuff, but perhaps there are advantages for you here – your teen might suddenly begin to wash his own sheets. And, remember, a shut door might need knocking upon from now on.

Let's get that picture out of your mind fast and move on.

# MARKS . . .

. . . are everything for some kids, while others just don't give a toss and some pretend not to care but do. A lot. You can coach them and STEM them and STEAM them but try to think about more than marks. Think about how hard they are striving. Think about their emotional intelligence, their ability to problem solve and their social skills – these are probably equally or more important to their long-term future than their marks (unless they want to study Medicine or Law and then, yes, marks are a huge focus of their teen years). Focus on trajectory – are they improving where once they were struggling? There's a film from 2013 on YouTube called 'The day I passed maths', featuring a teen who struggled with maths all through school, always getting F grades. He shows his dad his C grade. The dad yells and bursts into tears, and the teen is so thrilled and proud of himself and they hug and it's beautiful and it's worth all the As in the world to that family. Be that dad. We love that dad. That's an A plus in parenting right there (*see E is for Expectations*). Confidence can give an enormous boost in marks, so be careful with your words about marks and success.

And then there are other, much more scary, sorts of marks. If your child has marks on their body that look like self-harm, you need to talk to them about it and get them help. Now.

## MONEY

They want it. And we have it. Even when we don't. Don't let them take advantage here. They can get a job at 14 years and 9 months. It's harder than it used to be, but there are still some delivery jobs, kitchen work, shop work and dog walking and some amazing kids create great side hustles baking cupcakes or running an online business. Their own money can be used to pay for their hobbies and fashion obsessions.

## MIRROR

Mirrors are like crack for most teens. They are drawn to them like moths to a flame. It's not narcissism; it's about working out who they are and getting used to that rapidly changing face. Or it could be about popping pimples. Or about that gelled-up hairdo, or learning how to do make-up by watching endless tutorials on YouTube. Sometimes a lit room on a dark night provides the perfect giant mirror for them to dance, preen or watch themselves. It's kind of gorgeous. Of course, there are some who avoid mirrors and shrink from them like vampires from sunlight – these teens have our understanding and empathy.

If your teen uses windows for endless preening, tell them they'll be able to see their reflection better if they clean the windows first.

## MENTAL ILLNESS

In 2016 just under one in four young people aged 15–19 years who responded to an Australian Youth Survey met the criteria for having a probable serious mental illness. There has been a significant increase in the proportion of young people meeting this criteria over the past five years and this is, of course, terribly worrying. The complicated wirings of the brain can sometimes lead to short circuits. There are, of course, many other factors involved, including drugs, family history, abuse, neglect, pressure, stress and, many believe, social media (an area which is now being much researched). We understand how scary it is to go through this with a teen. But know that with early detection and intervention with the help of professionals, many young people will resolve their issues quickly.

So do get them to your GP if you are worried about them, especially if they stop enjoying the things that once gave them joy, if they are not sleeping and eating properly, if they're overly despondent and withdrawn or over-hyped and over-anxious. Encourage them to talk to you and, when they do, try to stay calm if they tell you they feel out of control.

Also, beware of the over-compliant child who pretends to be happy when they're actually struggling. We've all heard the terrible stories of teens who seemed fine and then disappear, or for the parents' worst nightmare to occur. If they feel they can be vulnerable with you, they will be less likely to hide their distress. Tell them that you might not be able to fix them instantly but you will do everything you can to get them the help they need. It might be medication, it might be counselling, it might be group therapy, but you will walk with them on the road to recovery and wellness and you will never leave their side.

If your child is in psychological distress, you have our love and our compassion, because watching the child you love struggle with mental illness is heartbreaking, terrifying, gruelling and overwhelming. Take time off from work if you can, and, please, take care of yourself. There are great resources such as kids' helplines, services such as Reach Out, and local health district programs for adolescent health. But there are also massive gaps in the system with a lack of psychiatric nurses, hospital beds and facilities. You will need to be their advocate and warrior to negotiate the system ahead.

Encourage your teen to tell you if they are worried about a friend, or if they have a friend who is behaving strangely, saying scary things about self-harm or posting threats to themselves or others on social media. We've heard of lives saved through the actions and concern of a teen friend who went to their parents and told them they were scared about a mate. Tell them they will not be in trouble if they reveal a friend might be in danger; indeed, they could be saving their life. Perhaps it's good to talk through scenarios. If your teen does reveal a friend's distress and you don't know the parents, tell the school counsellor. If it's on a weekend and you are really worried, call the emergency services and seek help.

N is for ... not listening

# N

## IS FOR . . .

NOT LISTENING,
NETFLIX, NUNYA

## NOT LISTENING

Teens rarely seem to be listening to you. They don't hear your questions about marks, requests to put out the garbage, or general inquiries. If you scream at them to hang out the washing on the line they will hear 'blah blah blah washing line'. This is due to their remarkable inbuilt filter that checks for tone of voice. We have evidence for this: one teen we know obviously registered something and went out and collected all the sopping wet clothes from the line and brought them inside, stepping over the laundry basket filled with other wet clothes on the way. Teen dreaminess.

But sometimes they actually *are* listening. Your beliefs, values, fears and furies are getting through, even when it seems the teen is a brick wall. Those fights with your partner? They hear them. That threat to move, because you're worried about the mortgage, the new motorway or climate change? That scares them. Those complaints about them behaving like a horror? They sense it. So be careful what you say.

## NETFLIX

If you don't have it, you are condemning them to a life of being left out of the conversation. Besides, there's some great stuff for you to watch too. But instead of all hanging in your separate rooms watching separate screens, you could try something radical like 'watching something together'. Consider it bonding time, but it can be even more important than that. There are controversial shows, such as 13 Reasons Why, that are part of the teen zeitgeist. If you ban such shows they might sneak and watch them alone, but if you watch with them you can give the perspective of an adult rational brain to help them process and make sense of what they've seen. This also helps them be critical consumers.

This post is not sponsored by Netflix, but if they'd like to send us some of their zillions we're up for it.

## NUNYA ...

... is what a friend's son says every time she asks him anything beyond: 'How was your day?' You might hear it a lot after your teenager turns 14. It means 'None of Your Business'. Direct questions don't work with teens; if you want to find out about their life, take the back door around things, listen when they chat to their friends in your car, take them for walks and 'shoot the shit'. That's when you get the real stuff. Because their life *is* your business.

O is for... over-identifying

# O

# IS FOR . . .

OVER-IDENTIFYING,
ORGANISATIONAL
SKILLS, OVERSCHEDULED,
ORTHODONTIC DEBT,
OTHER PARENTS

# OVER-IDENTIFYING

They are the best of you and you made them and they are fabulous. But they are not you. You can't live through them and you can't live again. Do not live your own fantasies through them. Most of us have crossed the line sometimes: finishing their Solar System model at midnight with superglue and a beer; proofreading their science project and adding a few 'suggestions' . . . But try not to do it too often. They won't get satisfaction from a job well done – and you won't get a good mark for that essay anyway and then you'll be really cross.

They are not your second chance at life – they are their own first chance. Over-identifying leads to anxiety for all of you.

There's some fascinating research about how much empathy you have for your teen. It shows that if you over-invest in compassion they will thrive; however, you will inflame your own health system and age prematurely. So, if you are feeling old and haggard at their 21st, know that you gave it your all.

# ORGANISATIONAL SKILLS

For many teens, this is the hardest skill to learn in high school. It's massive. Some of them take years and never get it. Teens need to learn to pre-plan, know their timetable, pack their bag, plan assignments and study for tests. It does seem the assignments and tests all come in the same week, leaving the week before that as scramble time. Some teens will take it in their stride (you lucky bastards), some will get hopelessly lost and confused and drop the ball (we're with you) and some will get themselves so over-organised that they become anxious. Don't organise for them, but help if they need it. Stationery is good. Highlighter pens are, too. Glue sticks are great. Not panicking is perfect. Expecting sudden skills is stupid. That fresh young teen brain just doesn't have the executive functionality that organisation and time management require. Help them set up good habits early – folders, calendars, study timetables and a desk they can actually see under all their stuff.

## OVERSCHEDULED

Today's teens are a busy bunch of kids. If your child has soccer on Monday afternoon, a music lesson on Monday evening, swimming and chess club on Tuesday, athletics and theatre sports on Wednesday, dance and debating on Thursday, two sessions of coaching on Friday, followed by film club and philosophy club and then a full weekend of organised fun, we say: 'Wow! What? Really? How you can afford it? How the hell do you get them to it all? And why aren't they, and you, hysterically over-stretched and cranky?'

Often the kids with this kind of schedule in year 7 will run out of steam and end up doing nothing by year 9. Let them chill and learn to juggle balls as well as life and schedules. At around 14 they might want to quit band or sport because 'it's for losers'. 'You will regret it' you will say, before trailing off when you realise you sound exactly like your mother and nothing has changed. Try to keep them doing a couple of activities for social, physical and mental health, but let them have some agency. It's great for them to try lots of activities and then whittle them down to those they most enjoy. Don't insist they only do stuff they are great at – let them do things they really suck at but enjoy; like dancing if they've got two left feet or swimming when they're never going to break any records.

# ORTHODONTIC DEBT

The braces take longer to pay off than the time they actually spend on the teeth. And they all seem to need them. One day you're at the dentist for a routine clean, the next day the orthodontist is asking pointedly if you're 'happy with your child's smile'.

'Yes,' you reply. 'I rarely see it, but when I do it's like a cold beer on a hot day, a shining light in the darkness of existence, a fire on the ice.'

The orthodontist will frown, lean forward and ask, 'Don't you care that it's lopsided?'

Their smile is gold to you, but to the orthodontist it's a new convertible.

Sometimes their jaw is off-kilter and might lead to issues with teeth wearing down, or being overcrowded. But do get a second opinion if you feel the braces are optional.

Your teen might be fitted with an expander plate that you have to wind wider every night with a spikey metal mini-torture-device. We had a friend who just couldn't do it. When her partner was away she would approach random strangers whose children also had expanders. They would stand over her son and wind his mouth wider while he lay down in the playground.

Many kids have braces these days and, God, they're brave . . . The metal in the mouth, the mortification, the catching on the lips, the pain after the braces are tightened, the ulcers, sores, metallic taste and yucky bits of food sticking in them is awful to endure. It's almost as painful as your debt and payment plan. But hopefully it will delay their sexual escapades while making them more beautiful for their straight-and-shiny-teethed future. Good luck, and may the debt be with you.

## OTHER PARENTS . . .

. . . can drive you crazy. You might be happy your teen is doing fine; that they're well adjusted, reasonably happy, getting decent marks and are pretty damn fabulous. And then you'll stand next to that parent at the year 10 barbecue who talks about their gifted teen's straight-A marks, selection for an International Opera School and future slot in the NASA space station. You slump. Then there's the taekwondo dad—coach whose kid is obviously going to the Olympics, who never chooses your kid for the team and who never stops telling you about the selective school test his boy aced. You might tell another parent that your kid finally passed her first maths test; they tell you their child has been chosen for the Maths Olympiad and International Young Diplomat scheme at the United Nations.

It seems every kid is a genius these days and it's almost hard to find an ordinary one. But be proud of your average kid. They're wonderful. Don't get psyched out by other parents. Who knows what they're covering up, and, even if they're not, we need all types of people in the world and we can't all be A-grade winners.

P is for... perfectionism

# P

## IS FOR . . .

PERFECTIONISM, POUT,
PIERCINGS, PERIODS,
PARTIES, PRIVACY,
PROCRASTINATION,
PARENT-TEACHER NIGHT,
PUSHING VS PULLING BACK,
PETS, PUBERTY, PORN, PHONE

## PERFECTIONISM

The teen who has to be perfect can be as worrying as the procrastinating, messy slob teen who doesn't get anything done. And sometimes the teen who can't get anything much done might actually be frozen by perfectionism and fear of failure. This is a rising phenomenon, particularly among young girls; recent research found 52 per cent of year 12 girls have clinical levels of anxiety. Perfectionism has been identified as a risk factor for anxiety, depression and eating disorders. Educators have raised the alarm over the problem, with the principal of a prominent British girls' school introducing a program called 'The death of Little Miss Perfect'. Schools in the US are also working on reducing perfectionism.

It's great if an adolescent is driven and ambitious, but sometimes this capability can go too far. An ambitious teen will be satisfied with doing well, but a perfectionist will see any small mistake as a failure. They might be hard on themselves and others, interpret a good mark as terrible, be constantly working, be extremely rigid in their thinking, be anxious and overly cautious, lack spontaneity, have body image problems and won't try new things in case of failure. Perfectionism can be the groundwork for mental health issues. Very competitive schools can be hotbeds of perfectionism and many are now doing clever things to help kids keep things in perspective. They teach teens how to cope with mistakes, to fail, to deal with rejection and to be critical thinkers in reference to the perfect lives they see portrayed on social media. And you can help them.

If you're really worried, take your child to a professional. And there are other things you can do along the way. Try not to use words like 'genius', 'perfect' and 'brilliant', nor constantly compare your kid to others; be unconditionally loving and caring, let them know it's ok to stuff-up. Admit your own mistakes and articulate what you learnt from them and how they helped you. Let them see you laugh off those stuff-ups, give yourself a break, and express delight in their hard work and improvement rather than their marks.

## POUT

The sulky pout of the teen who wants to flaunt their mood has been around since time began – presumably the pursed lips of the Paleolithic teenager can be detected in cave paintings. Yet the sexy trout pout for the camera is a recently domesticated variation that has now reached pestilence level. Don't ever let their grandparents follow them on Instagram, although many teens have two accounts – one for relatives, one for real people.

## PIERCINGS

If you've held off this long, you will be under pressure to allow piercings. You can refuse to pay, tell them how much it hurts, warn of infection and hospital visits and abscesses, but all this will be meaningless when they are anaesthetised with ice cubes by a good friend at a party, or pass a local chemist that has cute studs on sale. Your teen who snores through legal studies class will probably know the age they can get their ears pierced without your consent (usually 16).

You might remember the pain of your own piercings, but today's teens are tough and regard pain as weakness: they will boast that it only hurts in the cartilage. Let the school make the rules about it if you can't be bothered. Teens with dubious hygiene practices will need twice-daily nagging to clean the piercing and to take care of it. We know a smart teen who rang from Schoolies Week to tell her mum she'd got a face tattoo; when her mother stopped breathing she revealed she'd merely got a nose ring. The mother was so relieved she approved. Smart kid.

If you detest piercings, do remember that they can close up (belly buttons super-quickly) while tattoos are there for life. Tattoos are more likely to require your parental consent, depending on where you live. After that, you just have to hope they have your great taste.

## PERIODS

Periods might begin before your girl becomes a teen or perhaps not until towards the end of high school. That's a big range, but first menstruation most commonly occurs about two years after a girl develops breasts, so she and you need to be prepared. From that stage on make sure she has a little purse in her school bag with pads you have taught her how to use. Of course, it's most likely her first period will happen when you are away, or when she is away, or in the middle of a big swimming gala. Murphy of Murphy's law was a bloke after all.

She will have lessons in primary school that discuss menstru-ation, but the best attitude for you is openness all through childhood and lots of little conversations rather than one big one. The late bloomers will probably take it in their stride, but for many little girls their first period is not a joyful entry to womanhood. Don't make a huge fuss or song and dance about it. Don't tell her it means she can have babies now. She doesn't want babies. She wants a pad, a cuddle, some chocolate and possibly a hot water bottle. Tell her it means her body is working as it should and boys have other issues to deal with, such as unwanted erections. A little gift is a lovely welcome to 'becoming a woman'. She'll cringe but be comforted.

Periods can be anything from annoying to terribly painful and they mark a loss of freedom for many young girls. A pool party is no longer exciting; white pants, gymnastics and camping might lose their gloss. When she is ready for tampons she will use them, but some resist for years. The new period undies are exciting for many. Talk to your teen about not disposing of any sanitary products down the toilet and to be prepared for irregular periods, especially in the first few years. Some girls have terrible pain, or nausea or PMT and headaches. If this means she is withdrawing from activities, missing school or sleep, or struggling, take her to the GP for help. Periods shouldn't be hell.

## PARTIES

A party is very different to, and possibly more dangerous than, a 'gatho', but not as dangerous as a 'free'. A party should mean parents are at home – possibly hiding in the kitchen, but checking on things and hopefully using

What's that you're taking to the party?

A present.

friends and older siblings as bouncers and bag checkers. A 'free' means 'parent free'. This could go horribly wrong. A friend's teen went to a thumpin' free (a party with a DJ, dope, other drugs and definitely no one over 19); the adolescent who hosted had so much money that she had rented an Airbnb property with her own credit card. With 20 friends she had constructed an elaborate sleepover fabric of lies for the parents – this showed impressive organisational skills that must be admired on some level. But word got out and kids came from miles. The Airbnb got trashed. The kids got trashed. The parents' trust got trashed.

If your child gets invited to any kind of party, you need to ask questions that they may think are a gross intrusion on their privacy. Ask where the party is. Ask if there will be parents there. Ask for the parents' numbers. Call them. Ask the parents if they will be home and if they will be allowing alcohol. Ask if they will be searching bags. Don't do all this if your child is 18, but younger than that and you have a right to know. If we drop teens at a party we often like to go to the front door and meet the parents and stickybeak the house. We know we're weird like this – at many parties kids are dropped off and picked up without any parents appearing at all. If your child is going to a friend's place to get ready for a party, be aware this could involve sipping from a thermos containing vodka while shivering themselves blue in a dark park. This is 'preloading' and means they are half pissed when they arrive at the party, so they only need take a little bottle hidden in their bra (in case they are searched) to keep themselves going all night.

If you are hosting a party, you are brave and wonderful. It is your legal obligation to keep those kids safe. Ensure the party has not been posted on a public social media page, to reduce the chance of gatecrashers. If you supply alcohol to under 18s you can be charged. If you are going to host an eighteenth party and some kids are under the legal drinking age, consider giving their parents a waiver to sign. If they are all under 18 you should probably hire bouncers or rope in older children's friends. And you need to be there, not hiding under your bed or away. Don't stalk, but do walk around with water occasionally, check the presents, the garden and their bags for alcohol and patrol the bathrooms occasionally. Look out for unconscious kids; if you find one, turn them on their side and ring an ambulance. Lock up the bedrooms. If you go to sleep and wake up in a house covered in used condoms, vomit, vodka bottles and whipped cream canisters, your kid might be considered a legend but you may have failed. Make them clean it up. While hungover. Especially the vomit. Big life lessons.

## PRIVACY

This has become a thorny topic. We live in an age when parents can supervise their children from afar using location apps. This is useful, especially for those precious teens who have absolutely no sense of direction and frequently get lost. If they're out at night, it's good to know where they are, but you have to admit that following their every move is kind of weird. They might overuse the word 'stalking' (*see L is for Language*) but on this occasion, perhaps they're right. There's a line between appropriate supervision and inappropriate stalking and you need to draw it for yourself.

You're at a disadvantage here as they get older: teens are much smarter than us on the smartphone. They can get around the location apps, leave the phone somewhere, give it to someone else, turn it off and escape your tracking.

Giving them total privacy requires total trust. Few teens deserve total trust, yet they are entitled to some. Perhaps when they are in their bedroom alone – we're aware this means that if their computer is on the world is in there with them, with all its weirdness, creepiness and meanness. So keep an ear out, an eye on things and an open conversation about their behaviour.

In terms of their social media, stress to your teen to never post anything they wouldn't want a future employer or their granny to see. They should learn the opposite of what might feel natural – dance like no one is watching and private message as if it's going to be read out loud at assembly. See *S is for Social Media* for more on this.

## PROCRASTINATION

Why do now what you can put off until tomorrow? There are a million memes, group chats and songs screaming much louder for attention than their homework. Suggest some down-time and then an hour of homework when their mind is free. Putting it off just makes them feel worse. To help overcome procrastination, talk to them about managing time and not their mood. If they say they'll do it when they 'feel like it', point out that might not happen spontaneously (or before hell freezes over). Stress is not a good motivator.

Many teens can't plan the next day, let alone their homework assignments or their study timetable. And yet, amazingly, they can spend weeks planning a party, months planning the formal and years planning their gap year. It's uncanny.

## PARENT-TEACHER NIGHT ...

... is like speed dating on steroids. Most schools have five-minute windows and little can be said, learnt or done, except to note that a teacher seems lovely. Or not. It's a production line and perhaps more about making us feel good about our teenager than anything else. Generally, with schools, we reckon that no news is good news and you're unlikely to learn about major issues while chatting at breakneck speed with a row of parents jostling at your back, desperate for their go. Be ready, prepare by chatting to your child about their teacher and the subject, know what you want to ask, and be kind and courteous and respectful. Don't embarrass your child. (Sorry, we know that's almost impossible – but try.)

## PUSHING VS PULLING BACK

This is the existential question that looms as large in adolescence as the Theory Of Everything in the philosophy of science. Only parents can decide how much to shove and how much to retreat. We try to push our kids to do something they're slightly worried about, so they can gain a sense of accomplishment. We try and nudge them to activities that give them a skill in life, or at least a skill in discipline and commitment. But, then again, sometimes they dig in their heels and won't have a bar of it and that can be like pushing you-know-what uphill. Teens begin to work out what they want and what they like and their push back is part of growing up.

If you push them to do something too much, they might begin to hate it. As they grow older it's all about less push and more pull back from you. Let them start to make decisions, direct their path, decide their future. Pushing them to do medicine when they want to be an architect will not help them, or you, in the future (particularly if that wannabe architect ends up operating on you). Of course, retreating and pulling back too far might make them think you don't care. Let us know if you find the magic formula.

# PETS . . .

. . . are fabulous. They teach responsibility, capability and caring. They also offer unconditional love and don't tell the teen to sweep the yard and do their homework. After an awful day, let your adolescent lie in bed and tell the cat, dog or axolotl their woes. They can take the dog for a walk when they've given up on all other form of exercise. Or, better still, you can walk with them and the dog, which offers companionship but not face-to-face inquisition. It's now been proven that the presence of a calm dog reduces the stress hormone cortisol – hence the use of companion dogs in court cases and other stressful situations. Playing with a calm pup also increases oxytocin – the love hormone that makes people feel less anxious. So an all-in cuddle on the bed with your teens and a pet might be crowded and smelly but it gives all of you a natural oxytocin high. It also gives everyone a reason to be close without having to voice that they need it. You might have limits to how far you will take this – fair enough if your teen never gets the ferret or python they want while living in your house.

And there's another reason for getting a pet. You. When your teen is surly and withdrawn and you need a cuddle, the dog will love you adorably, completely and endlessly.

## PUBERTY

This is a major transformation of body, mind and spirit. Imagine going to bed one night and waking up measurably taller. Their arms seem too long and suddenly they can feel like a stranger in their own skin. The boobs, the pubes, the pimples, the muscles can all come as a shock. Know that this is freaky for them and it's freaky for you. Seeing your son transform into a man is just incredibly weird; even though you know it's coming, you are never really ready for it. Suddenly, instead of climbing into your lap they are giving you bone-crushing hugs or thrashing you in a friendly game of basketball. Seeing your daughter get checked out on the street is creepy and confronting.

Mothers, it has now been officially proven that when puberty aligns with menopause you have what is medically termed a 'clusterfuck'. They are blossoming and blooming while you are pruning and decaying. They are bleeding as you stop. But their emotional pain is real and yours is not allowed. If this is happening in your home, you have our sympathy. Perhaps use it to understand their feelings. Perhaps we have more in common with teens than we think.

**PORN** (*See X is for X-rated* because this one is big, awful and confronting so it needs some space.)

## PHONE

Many teens get a smartphone when they start high school. To go without might see them viewed by their peers as a member of a weird cult. Phones are useful; teens often travel alone to school so it's practical to be in touch, look up train timetables and stare at when they don't want to make eye contact beyond their fringe. But, just because your child has a phone, don't think they know that it is an actual phone. You think a phone is for talking. You are wrong. Your teen probably won't answer calls and they won't make calls. This means when you call them to ask which train they're on, it will go to a default voicemail or ring out. If you text them, zilch. But if you are not there at the station to pick them up, they will text instantly:

mum where r u? I'm waiting in the cold!!! 😠 😠 😠 😠 😠

A phone is not a phone to them: it's a mini computer. And if they use it for text they don't think like you. Their texts will

be a one-line message

then another line message

then another line message

Such as:

i dont want to do NAPLAN

please

it sux

can I skip it?

why arent you answering me

muuuuuum ?????

dont dead read me

They text like this because of how they read texts. It's just too exhausting for them to open a message. But if *their* message isn't opened it's called a dead read and that may cause conniptions.

Teens' thumb dexterity is the next stage of evolution. First, we had primates with opposable thumbs, then *Australopithecus afarensis*, then *Homo sapiens* and now we have a generation with thumbs that can move like lightning, composing commentary and messages in real time. This makes them very dexterous. Teens can type antiauthoritarianism without looking. Don't try this yourself.

It is well documented that teens who use their phone excessively are more prone to disrupted sleep, restlessness, stress and fatigue. Yet no one has defined exactly what 'excessively' is. Phones are bad for anyone's brain, including yours. But the phone's utterly compelling nature and the growing teen brain makes it even harder for them to resist. We support schools that bother to do the deep messy working of teaching healthy digital habits that involve understanding their brains and how tech is designed to be unputdownable. We also get that bans are imposed in frustration. We understand the need for teens to self-regulate, but if you've picked up your own phone while reading this book you'll know how hard that is. We're all losing our focus, but they haven't even had time to develop theirs. Teens need space from their phones during the day and assistance in developing concentration techniques, but they won't learn to self-regulate without the opportunity to practise those skills. Try to ground them in the reality that's around the phone, not in it.

Q is for ... queer

# IS FOR . . .

QUEER,
QUARRELLING,
QUIET,
QUESTIONS

# QUEER

Queer is an identity. Teens who come out as queer are refusing to fit within the neat tight confines of sexuality and/or gender. To put it officially, queer is an umbrella term for sexual and gender minorities who are not heterosexual or cisgender. It doesn't mean they are gay or trans, but it can (*see T is for Trans*). It might just mean they are refusing to wear pink and be ultra-feminine for girls, or refusing to be boofy and blokey for boys.

It's often a stance they take if they are still deciding about their sexuality or just don't feel 'normal' (whatever that is). Teens are primed to explore, and increasing numbers are refusing to conform to narrow stereotypes.

Your teen is growing up in a time of great change in terms of gender and sexual identities. They are seeing and absorbing this more than you are. Male celebrities such as Billy Porter are wearing dresses to the Oscars, razor ads feature trans teens learning to shave with their dads and, generally, it's hip to be queer. This can bring family friction in traditional homes and is perhaps where the generation gap looms large. Grandparents find it even more confusing. You might need to help grandparents deal with a queer teen. (Remind them about the Scottish kilt and Elizabethan fashion.)

If your teen pronounces themselves queer, gay, bi, trans or questioning, know that it might have taken enormous bravery to tell you. Don't interrogate them, tell them 'it's a phase', or project your worries. You can hire a psychiatrist to try to change their mind, but it's likely they will charge you a day's wages to tell you that your child is, indeed, queer. But do see your GP and get a referral if they are really struggling, self-harming, or acting out with risky behaviour. And if you need family therapy or your own therapy or a support group to come to terms with this change, then do it. But keep your struggles private; this is not about you.

Travel this road with them. But let them be aware that in certain parts of their own country and overseas a queer teen will probably not be celebrated. In some countries they will even be breaking the law. This is sad and scary, but true.

## QUARRELLING

(*See also A is for Argumentative.*) It's sport to them that they don't necessarily want to play but just can't stop. You're like an itchy scab; they just need to pick at you until you bleed. It's tough to know when to play dead and when to get into the ring with them. You don't want to be endlessly fighting, but you also don't want to be a pushover. Set the quarrel to a few rounds and ding yourself in and out. Fight fair; don't use guilt, shame or condescending laughter. If they (or you) get hugely upset and flustered, call time. They can't think clearly when roused like that and chances are you can't either.

## QUIET

This used to mean they were asleep, reading or doing art. It was once a time of parental relief and a 'cup of tea, a Bex and a good lie down'. Now you cannot relax. Quiet time now usually means they are on social media and absorbing who knows what. So check in on an over-quiet teen. They might not be safe just because they're in their bedroom. Online safety is important – they need to be wise to the creeps and cretins who can prey on them.

But do let your adolescent have quiet down-time. There's interesting research about how over-scheduled they've become, so schedule in some nothing. Time for them to stare at the stars or the photos on their wall, time to sew, or redecorate, or draw, or write putrid poetry. We all need quiet in a world of haste and hustle. Enjoy some down-time with them. Buy a hammock and model how to swing in silence while watching the breeze moving the trees.

# QUESTIONS

It feels as if we question our teens a lot. But they are selectively deaf to our curiosity. You might start off with a chatty afternoon opener: 'Have you done your homework? How is your friend who was feeling a bit sad and overwhelmed? How are you feeling? Have you sent your Insta streaks today?' Only one of these questions – the last one – might get a grunt. You are most likely questioning air. Sometimes you will feel like a ghost in your own home.

Don't keep going. Give up until they come to you with a question.

'When's dinner?'

Then you can answer, 'After you tell me how your day was'.

Or, 'Can I have some money?'

'After I know if you've done your homework.'

Cruel, annoying, yet highly effective.

R is for... righteous
indignation

# R

# IS FOR . . .

RIGHTEOUS INDIGNATION,
RITUALS, RESILIENCE,
RELATIONSHIPS,
RISK-TAKING, RITALIN

# RIGHTEOUS INDIGNATION

Sometimes every sentence a teen utters is like a weapon of righteous superiority and, at times, it can make you feel under full missile attack. For people who are still so small in life experience, they can be bloody high and mighty. There they are, up on their podium, and there's you down below – small, stupid, insignificant and always wrong.

But sometimes we adults deserve a bit of righteous fury directed at us. We have some sympathy for teens and their righteous indignation when it comes to guns, violence, inequality, poverty, climate change and the future. The US teens of the Parkland school shooting made the world listen to their indignation with their speeches and brave, pithy, furious and sorrowful social media posts, including 'I'm not a Russian computer, so I can't vote' and the inadequacy of 'thoughts and prayers' from their President. You must admit some of the climate change protest signs are pretty pithy too.

A record number of 'just 18s' enrolled to vote in Australia's same-sex marriage plebiscite, but a record number then abstained from the general election. Tell them they can't whine and be righteous if they don't participate in the democratic process. Citizens have rights and responsibilities, so they need to educate themselves, sort through the lies, Russian bots and fake news and work out the future they want to vote for when they turn 18. Otherwise they are just pissing in the wind.

And if they ask what you are doing to secure a better future (and, chances are, they will), you need to be ready with your answers. Are you living an ethical life? Are you helping or hurting their future? Tell them to go and sort the recycling and compost, keep their showers to two minutes, and reduce their online time and electricity use to do their part. That will spur them on or shut them up.

## RITUALS

We're a bit jealous of cultures that have rituals. Rituals give a sense of belonging and can make the transition from childhood to adulthood something special rather than something embarrassing. The Bar Mitzvah, Bat Mizvah, Confirmation and the good old Debutante Ball fill this role beautifully – and the kids get great presents. If none of these rituals are your thing, perhaps you can create your own.

Only do what your teen is open to. There are coming-of-age rituals, camps and retreats if they are up for it. Your daughter might want her, or your, best girlfriends around for afternoon tea to welcome the beginnings of womanhood and community. Your son might want something similar. There are plenty of organised 'boys to men' camping trips and activities for fathers and sons and increasingly similar coming-of-age retreats for mothers and daughters. They are pretty gender defined, sometimes religious or new age by nature, but if that's your thing, why not? If it's not your jam then you could organise your own camping and hiking trips, but warn them the tent does not have a phone charger and there's no Wi-Fi in the bush.

But don't go overboard. When one friend's daughter got her period, the mother suggested a ritual with friends to celebrate. The teen ran away so fast she broke the land speed record. This should be a time of celebration and community, and not retreat. But should and could can be worlds apart.

You can design your own weekly rituals. Pizza nights, device-free dinners and seasonal barbecues are low-key but can still give a sense of connection and comforting coming togetherness.

# RESILIENCE . . .

. . . is the buzz word of modern parenting. And it makes perfect sense. The accepted wisdom is that we've given kids too many medals for just showing up and sitting up straight and the teen years are time to harden them up for adulthood. But resilience is not a hardening: it's a massaged muscle of self-care and a group of behaviours that will help them cope with the inevitable challenges ahead. They need to be assisted through difficulties in an increasingly hands-off way

as they traverse the teen years. Consult, assist, give feedback, but let them find a way through things. The more coping skills they develop, the better their wellbeing.

Resilience is mostly developed by experiencing a bump in the road and then refined by having to navigate something out of the ordinary and uncomfortable. If you prepare the road too perfectly for them by removing all obstacles, you are taking away the opportunity for them to become more resilient. As hard as it is to watch teens go through tough times, we cannot sanitise them against all emotional germs. Resilience is developed by encountering problems and then having positive attitudes, being optimistic, regulating emotions and learning to cope with failure. It requires a development of emotional intelligence, flexible thinking and a willingness to ask for help. Sometimes it's hard to know whether to give them a big kiss or a mighty kick up the bum. Helping them help themselves is the best way to think about it.

# RELATIONSHIPS

You might not even know your child is in a relationship. If it's forged at school it can just be a school affair, or it may begin online. Hopefully, you will get an inkling that love and lust is in the air. Many relationships begin with a love heart like on Instagram and then progress to endless hours of Facetime. They might not consider it a big deal – it might be sweet and fun – or they may be head over heels. Whatever it is, relationships are a responsibility and they matter.

Teens have a lot of rules about relationships. There are rules about who can go out with whom, who they can talk to when they're in a relationship, how long until they kiss, how they flirt, and who they can 'tune' with. Tuning comes before flirting, which comes before dating, which comes before a relationship. Dating can be via technology for weeks before they even meet. They have the capability to chat for ages or might just do their homework individually while looking at each other on their phone or computer. If they live far apart and don't spend much time together, be aware that this is when the sexy photo or nude selfie could crop up.

Your teen might not want to talk to you about their relationship. They could tell you to butt out. But in the car, when you are watching the road and they are watching their phone, you can chat about relationships in general. About the responsibility of holding another person's heart in their heart, about the negotiations required to decide how much time they spend together, both face to face and online. You can workshop the expectations each of them has of the partnership. Expectations are an interesting point – your teen might have a girlfriend or boyfriend who expects a lot more emotional maturity and intensity than they are capable of. Sometimes teens are in love with the idea of love; they've watched all the movies and want far more than another teen can offer. Then there are all those other relationship issues – if they are ready, if they're as into their girl/boyfriend as their partner is into them, and how serious they are. Relationships are tricky enough, but when you don't quite know who you are and what you want in life, then they can quickly get messy.

But we've got to be soppy here and point out just how gorgeous young couples are while in the first blush of love. Being close to two teens who are hot for each other is adorable and powerful – you can almost light a match with the barely repressed passion. First love is magnificent, brutal, wonderful and crushing. Their intensity is incredible; their desire to constantly touch means they look like chimps checking one another's hair for nits. But the heartbreak can be horrific. Teens can't anticipate that the feeling won't last forever and can be crazed with grief and shock when it's over. Don't just say 'you will love again'; try to understand their pain. Helping them develop self-care is vitally important here. They will need a lot of your love, affection and help to navigate the heartbreak. It will remind you of your own first love and loss and it will hurt in so many ways.

Don't diss a fangirl crush either: they are safe, intense affairs from afar that are bewildering and bonding. Mothers, remember how you loved so large?

Relationships mean you will most definitely have to have the sex talk. Make a cup of tea and turn to *S is for Sex*. But, think about this as you add the sugar: where do you want them doing it?

## RISK-TAKING

This might or might not be combined with relationships. Or it could be combined with many things. Your child is bursting with impulse. Acting on those impulses feels so good that the consequences can barely register. It's back to the brain-as-guilty-party here – it hasn't quite developed planning, control and forethought. Instead, it's hungry for that rush of feeling good and the reward of being admired by others and being part of a group.

Common risk-taking activities include experimenting with alcohol and drugs, having unprotected sex, wagging school, or getting in the car with someone who has been drinking or taking drugs. Be alert to this and perhaps try to encourage the types of risk-taking that will give them a different kind of high. Sport or activities (high ropes, abseiling) or hobbies they can try that are challenging and healthy.

It's also important to set up consequences for dangerous risk-taking: a curfew for social outings, and boundaries that grow with them and contract when they cross them. Life is about weighing up risks and learning how to make sensible decisions about when to take them.

You can't remove all risk, but you can help them learn which risk is worth taking and which is not. This comes back to attitudes shared in everyday conversations and perhaps practising scenarios you can dream up or that you hear about. Chatting to them while they are in a calm state about something they might encounter while out in groups means they can practise using the rational brain to override the need for speed or risk-taking.

# RITALIN

Ritalin is a drug prescribed for ADHD, which can dramatically help teens with the disorder to focus and sit still.

Some really need it.

The only problem is that a big black market has developed for this little white pill. Some teens might take what they call 'skittles' or 'smarties' to focus, study hard and even recover from parties. During the final years of school your teen might start to hear about the wonders of Ritalin as a performance-enhancing drug, and be begging you to take them to the doctor for a prescription. Hose it down, unless they really do have ADHD, because it's a medicine, not a drug of choice. There have been media articles referring to Ritalin as 'kiddy cocaine', which sounds rather tabloid-frenzied but the drug does act on the brain in a similar way. It's all about the neurotransmitter dopamine, which enhances cell-to-cell transmission of information.

Do not steal your child's Ritalin, no matter how tempting. It's not a good look for them to bust you at 3am on your PowerPoint productivity hack, despite your need for speed and your endless exhaustion. This is prescription only, people.

There are other smart drugs of choice for university students. Some research in the United States suggests up to 30 per cent of students at some colleges are taking them. These teens see smart drugs as a study aid; we see them as cheating, and health-care researchers see them as 'risky'.

Tell your teen that taking Ritalin recreationally can lead to changes in brain chemistry associated with sleep disruption and risk-taking behaviour. Snorting the drug for faster uptake can lead to a pattern of abuse and addiction.

Offer an occasional coffee and choc-chip cookie to stimulate their sleepy brain.

S is for...screen time & social media

# S

## IS FOR . . .

SCREEN TIME AND SOCIAL
MEDIA, SMELL, SQUAD,
SPORT, SEX, SEXTING,
SHOPPING, SHOPLIFTING,
STRESS, SINGLE PARENTING,
SOCIALISING, SCHOOLIES

## SCREEN TIME AND SOCIAL MEDIA

Today's teens' lives are drenched in media, and they make much of that media themselves.

The accepted wisdom is they are addicted to their screens. But that's like saying a drug addict is addicted to their syringe. They might be very dependent on what they are accessing on those screens, and the social cachet, connection and entertainment that provides. But so are you. In fact, recent research found teens are more worried about their parents' phone use than their own. We are all slightly ADHD today, thanks to our screen smorgasbord. A study by Common Sense Media, a non-profit children's advocacy and media ratings organisation, surveyed 500 pairs of parents and teenagers. They discovered parents are feeling increasingly addicted and 40 per cent of teens worry that their parents are total screen junkies. So, if you've checked Twitter, read three other articles and posted on Instagram while perusing this paragraph, get off your phone and show them the way. (The study also came to some worrying conclusions about sleep – *see Z is for Zzzzzz*.)

They are the screen generation. They need iPads and computers for schoolwork and these have become unavoidable in life, even if you chose Steiner schooling. You need to set limits, because they can rarely do that on their own. Help them, and while you are there, get them to help you. Some families insist on screens being kept under lock and key, like contraband. They set strict limits and conditions. They monitor screen time and social media use with apps (this can be eye opening). Warning: some kids hack these apps and can bring down the family Wi-Fi. Sucked in, parents! Now you can't sneak online either.

Games and social media light up the brain like gambling. You need to set limits. For gaming, that could involve the violence of the content, the length of time spent playing, the understanding that their language stays non-toxic and their sleep is not compromised. Take the controller away if they break those rules. They will suffer withdrawal symptoms like their grandparents did when they gave up smoking, but they will thank you for it. And when you have a gaming hiatus, all sorts of nostalgic old friends will reappear – boardgames, the dusty old football, conversation. It won't be easy – you might have to get off your phone to play Monopoly.

They are also the social generation. Social media ('soche') is Instagram, Snap(chat), TikTok, Omegle, Tumblr and all the trillion others that will have been created while this book was printing. Indeed, there were probably five new apps created between this word . . . and this one. You need to understand that social media is *very important*. For example, if your child does daily 'streaks' then you cannot take them out of the range of Wi-Fi for more than 24 hours. A streak is like a virtual wee on a post for a dog. It is their shout-out into the void that is the social space; if a streak ends then they have to start again. If you take them on a long plane trip or to a remote area and they can't streak, they might never talk to you again. It cannot be long before a teen wakes from a coma and screams that they missed a streak.

Many parents worry that social media is damaging to teens' brains, psyches and self-respect. The number of followers they have and how many likes they get seems way too important to them. They need to learn who their friends really are and understand that, while they might get a zing of delight and pleasure from each new like and each new follower, it's not healthy for them in the long run. However, don't panic: recent studies suggest we are overestimating how damaging social media actually is. And, besides, memes are hilarious. Many older teens come around to understand they are more than their likes and loves on any particular post. Healthy habits and improved media literacy will help your teen unpack and understand their social media feeds.

It can be confronting for parents when their teen starts to preen and shoot sexual pouty photos for their Instagram feed. (We are prudish old bags and don't like it at all.) If your 13-year-old is taking photos of herself in her bra or bikini and posting to social media, it's time to have a talk to her. She will say everyone else does it, and if you look at her feed it may indeed seem that way. We wouldn't advise you to ban it, but check she has a private account, understands all the settings and *really* knows all the people who follow her – point out they should be *real* friends, not 'Insta' friends. Then pray to Kim and Kanye that she gets over it soon. (*See K is for Kardashian feminism.*)

Always be aware of online or cyber bullying. And that other teens can be disgusting and cruel especially under the guise of a fake account or an anonymous app where there is no eye contact. So can creepy adults pretending to be teens. You want your teen to talk to you and tell you if they are being bullied on social media. Keep an eye out for changes in behaviour or an even more obsessive checking or sudden withdrawal from their phone. They won't tell you anything if they think you will take their phone away, so make sure you are ready to listen and respond and not react by throwing the damned thing in the bin. There are government safety websites for reporting procedures and more detailed advice.

Teens need to learn to screenshot, block, report and deal with the darkness. If it all gets too much they can get off social media. It sounds as if a lot of teens are rejecting social media for this reason and going low-fi.

But remember social media is also about socialising and all-important connection. For some teens, especially those in small towns or who haven't found their tribe, it can be a lifeline; a place they can practise social interactions, coach themselves to be more dynamic and assertive, and try out different ways of interacting. They can often express themselves more fully online, without the awkwardness they feel in real life. For those who are isolated and feel friendless, there can be others just like them to be found. You need to understand social media might be vital for your teen and banning it might make them more isolated.

Be aware there are strict unwritten codes for posting that you can't possibly understand. These document how often to post, who to follow and what to say. Whatever you do, *do not* follow their friends and comment on their posts. Do not post 'omg u soo cute I luv u' to a girl in their year you've known since preschool; you have just caused social death to them. And *never* message their friends on social media saying 'Don't be mean to Ella' or demanding: 'Why did you let Josh down over that assignment?' Resist. Always resist.

And what about your own social media? Don't post pics or stories about them once they've turned 15 without their permission.

Be careful about how they're identified and what location apps are on your own phone if you put them in your posts.

# SMELL

Wow – it's the waft of something sweet, or perhaps the stink and stench of something odious. The richness of the bouquet when it's all combined; those heady layers of sweat, bubblegum, deodorant, greasy hair, cheap perfume, lipgloss, shampoo, old socks, young blood. It's intoxicating, isn't it?

A teen's room also has its own strong smell that is unique. And odious as much as odorous. We talked about this in *B is for Bedroom*, but it's all about their endocrine system and body odour. Girls are not excluded here. You might have to repeat this mantra every night for at least six years: 'Clothes in the dirty clothes basket *now*, especially socks and sports gear.' Teach them to strip the bed every week and put on fresh sheets that you wash and dry in the sun's disinfecting rays. Insist on hair washing twice a week. Open their blinds to let the sunshine in (unless they are in bed, in which case they will shriek like a vampire). A humidifier can help. Forbid food in their room (yes, we know this is an argument to the death, but you are on the side of all that is good here). Of course, if their room is such a pigsty that you can't see the floor to vacuum or the bed to change it, then you might need to resort to some bribery, corruption and nagging. Pocket money can be conditional.

To combat odour, vacuum regularly and give carpets a good steam clean occasionally. Do the same with floorboards and the bed mattress. Use a mattress cover. Know this gross fact: people secrete over 95 litres of sweat into their beds each year. Teens may secrete more – it can be a sweaty time. Be nice: they might be helping you wash your sheets when you get really old and smelly.

## SQUAD

The squad is their friendship group. Sometimes it matters more than you. If there is trouble in the squad, there is trouble for you. Those fellow teens are the arbiters of all that is good, cool, fun and stupid. (*See F is for friends.*)

## SPORT

Sport is important. It's good for teens to get fit, keep active, get their heartrate up and have the social interaction that sport can bring. If they are sporty it also brings enormous self-confidence, kudos and muscles. Physical activity is not just good for their body, it also has a strong influence on mental wellbeing. Getting active reduces stress and anxiety and improves their self esteem. Unfortunately, a lot of teens quit sport around year 9 or 10. They start getting bored of it, feel lethargic and don't want to get up early in the morning for practice. Try to encourage them to keep going or to try a different sport or physical activity – a dance class, barre class at the gym, ice skating … Something non-competitive that takes the pressure off and brings joy, a rise in heartrate and better mental health. Or join a gym yourself and try to drag a teen in as a guest a couple of times a week. Or run them around the park with a dog. If you don't have a dog, consider borrowing one.

Then, of course, there are the super-sporty kids who are elite level and wouldn't dream of quitting. Those dynamos who play rep or swim four days a week like powerful machines following that black line on the bottom of the pool, or the soccer stars who train four times a week and play two games every weekend, do sport camps in the holidays and get selected for international competitions. You must be proud of them. They need a lot of food as fuel, a lot of driving, a lot of sacrifice on your part. You might worry they're doing too much at times – and indeed they may. All that growing and puberty takes a lot of energy and they can get over-exhausted, especially when training conflicts with schoolwork. If your teen is too tired and emotional for practice, sometimes it's understandable. But it's probably more likely to be the other way around – pumped for practice but too tired for school. What is the ultimate aim here? The Olympics? Scholarships? The National Ballet? Or enjoying being in their body, fitness, good mental health and setting up healthy patterns for adulthood? They might have a dream of playing for their country, but talk to them about a back-up course or trade in case it doesn't work out or they have to retire at 22.

And, remember, every medal they win: it's part yours! When they're asleep, hang it around your neck and bite down on that gold. You're a champ.

And, when you're on the sidelines, behave. It's not your game.

## SEX

We know you don't want to think about this, but it *will* happen at some stage.

Tell your kids it's illegal until they're 16 and, even then, it comes with a lot of responsibility and side effects. Also talk to them about what's legal in terms of age difference. (*See C is for Consent.*) You can try to delay their sexual starting date with legal warnings, but you should also be

realistic if they look like they are becoming sexually active.

A recent study by La Trobe University surveyed more than 6300 Australian students in years 10, 11 and 12. It found the onset of sex had been getting later but actually dipped back down to a younger age again in 2019. Thirty four per cent of year 10 students had had sex (it was 27 per cent in 2013). The National Survey of Australian Secondary Students and Sexual Health discovered three-quarters of teens aged between 15 and 18 were sexually active in some way, including oral sex, deep kissing or genital touching. Unsurprisingly, the teens were pretty happy about it (their parents may not have been so thrilled). The good news is that most were having sex at home and 62 per cent had only had one partner in the past year. Nearly 80 per cent said they protected their sexual health by using condoms.

You probably had a sex education teacher who showed the class how to slide a condom onto a banana? Now, 80 per cent of teens use the internet for sex education. They have hard-core porn at their fingertips (*see X is for X-rated*) and this means they might already know more than you do about certain sex acts. Yet, they might *not* know about how to give pleasure, how to initiate sexual interaction, consent, safety and diseases. Talk about pleasure and how anal sex is not mandatory and is not 'cool'. Talk about porn sex verses real sex, and the different types of porn sex: some is bleached butt holes and Brazilians, while some is homemade. None of it is necessarily useful in learning to be a caring lover when they are ready for sexual relationships.

Also, you need to have the condom talk. Yes, you do. And you may well need to show them how to use the condom, and even show them with a banana. We remember hearing Whoopi Goldberg talking about her daughter getting pregnant at a young age. She asked her, 'Didn't you use a condom?' Her daughter answered: 'I did, and we washed it out carefully each time.' Doh.

The doing it in the car versus at home is the other thing you need to think about. Sexual safety is more than just disease and pregnancy; kids sneaking around in dark parks at night are simply not safe. Home is safer. And don't ever assume a closed door with two people behind it means studying. They could be going for it big time. We know parents who run up and down stairs all day opening doors.

Teens need to know that sex will change their relationship. It will become more intense. You will worry about what this means if they break up in the middle of important exams. But we've observed a lot of long, intense and loving sexual relationships among older teens that have been impressive in their maturity and kindness.

If your child is in a relationship and wants to spend a lot of time behind closed doors in your house or have sleepovers with their lover, then you need to have a conversation with the other parents. How do they feel about it? State how you feel about it. If one family allows sleepovers and the other doesn't, then you have some differences to discuss. Some might be happy to leave their teen alone for a week with an open invitation for others to join the party. Others watch their child closely and would be devastated if they had sex in your house. How do you feel about it? Possibly sick. We get it. Rarely ready for it? That goes without saying.

Teens ready for a sexual relationship will take any opportunity they can, but be aware that opportunity could be dodgy and dangerous. Be aware of the sleepover tree where teens construct elaborate alibis.

If you have an adult teen living at home and you'd love them to move out, then impose a no-sex rule. Your house, your rules.

This is confronting stuff. We've heard of parents stepping on a used condom, retching and then ringing to make an appointment for therapy.

## SEXTING

This is sending sexy or sexually explicit photos or messages on message apps. The same La Trobe study above, showed the sexting craze is slowing down. In 2013 more than 70 per cent of sexually active year 10–12 students had sent explicit texts, and 84 per cent had received them. Thanks to better education and a realisation of how it can all go horribly wrong, that's down to one in three sending and half receiving. Most of the time, these are sent to a girlfriend or boyfriend, but they do need to understand a message can be screenshot and shared with friends when the relationship is over – this is revenge porn (the sharing of sexually explicit photos or videos of someone without their permission).

One in 10 Australians have had a nude image distributed without their consent. There are criminal codes that make this illegal; different states and countries have different laws with different penalties but no legislation will be enough to completely stamp it out. The victims feel shame, horror and embarrassment, and teens need to understand the risk they take and responsibility they have. Be aware some young people might think sexting is fun and empowering and they simply don't understand your angst. It's almost become a new base in sexual experimentation. We've heard of relationships where there's texting, sexting and then meeting. It's physically safer but there are massive ramifications if there's revenge or a lack of respect for privacy. There's definitely a generation gap on this topic.

Some young teens are so aware of the power of their sexual image that they even sell pictures of themselves online. They will do that under a different account, so don't assume the account you know about is the only one they have. It might seem like the end of the world if this happens, but remember, they are not the only one. Shut it down immediately. It might also be illegal, depending on their age and the nature of the photo.

Millennials have been the guinea pigs in terms of sexting and social media, so a smart Millennial might be the best person to talk to and warn your teen. Be aware that society will change with the generations and your teen will probably one day have a Millennial boss with an intimate tattoo that the entire company has seen.

## SHOPPING

A lot of kids love shopping. Just not with their mothers. Shopping centres are usually safe places to chill with their friends, window shop, eat crap food, watch movies and be silly. Some shops play Barry Manilow to scare them away, but soon the teens will find that ironic–cool and the tactic will backfire.

## SHOPLIFTING

There could be shoplifting at some point. This is a teen thing more common in some groups than others. In some schools it's almost a rite of passage. You can wait for a call from store security or pre-warn them if you have a hunch it's happening. If they come home with stuff they can't afford or make jokes about shoplifting, talk to your adolescent about security cameras, a criminal record, juvie and not being able to ever go to that place again.

## STRESS

Everyone seems stressed these days. We're all just so damn busy and overwrought and that means life is stressful for us and it's stressful for them. They might have less responsibility than you, but they've got different types of stresses and stressors. Imagine not knowing what you're good at and who you are, what you are becoming, where you belong, what you're going to do, and then waking up different every day. Add to that the need to fit in and have friends and get good marks and be good at sport and know what's cool on Netflix at the moment. Spice that up with endless exams, assignments and parental pressure.

Acknowledge they can be stressed and you can help model how to deal with it all. Show them how *you* deal with stress – no, not the Riesling. Put that down! We're talking about the exercise, the breathing, the mindfulness meditation sessions, the yoga, the plenty of sleep, and the fun music blasting in the car when you need to lift your spirits. Stress is different to anxiety: it's temporary and it's a state, rather than a way of being in the world. But for some teens it can become a way of being and reacting to everything and they will need your help to stay calm.

If you feel your teen is genuinely overloaded with stress and can't face school, you might want to consider a mental health day at home if you can take one off to be with them. Or a day off Saturday sport for you both to enjoy. Suggest they do a five-minute meditation with the help of an app, a big walk or a visit to the gym to get the endorphins firing. You could make brownies together and snuggle on the sofa with a funny movie. Sometimes it's best to retreat from school work and social interaction to just declutter their brain. Let home be their sanctuary, their place of retreat from the stress of life. It will make them feel safer and more secure and give them a shell to escape to. But if your home is full of stress and you are all struggling to cope, help them find other retreats.

# SINGLE PARENTING

A special shout-out to you single parents. You deserve that week in a resort when your child finishes school! You are going through every one of these topics alone, unassisted and often unappreciated. Even worse, there's no one you can throw all your frustration at, share the pain with, or download the drudgery to. It's intense and, at times, insane. We see you, we know you, we salute you. We feel you should always be served first in queues, skip the customs line at airports and get the first biscuit when the packet is opened. We hope you get help from a friend who is close to your teen, perhaps a fairy godmother or father or grandparents. We hope you have a parents/school group for support and understanding. We hope you swim laps and scream underwater occasionally. And we know this: your grumpy, surly, sarcastic teen will salute you one day. They will honour your incredible hard work and appreciate your stoicism.

If you are recently separated, try not to let your teen play you off against each other and exploit any disagreements about parenting between you. Try to negotiate a mutual agreement about things such as homework, sleepovers, dating, money and chores. If you are part of a smug couple and you know a single dad finding it tough, offer to help his daughter go shopping for a formal dress. If you know a single mum who can't do multiple simultaneous sport drop-offs, offer lifts to her teen and access to your dinner table. Teens need a village.

# SOCIALISING

In some ways this generation seems hyper-social and connected. But in terms of face-to-face socialising, well, frankly, a lot of them need to do it more. Many parents are pushing their teens to go out, and even organising play dates for young people up to the age of 19! This is an inside generation. You can help by suggesting school holiday camps, art classes, movies, picnics or visiting galleries; activities that aren't screen-based. Do encourage socialisation – it's important for life skills. But don't worry about the late bloomers: they will eventually get social; probably during their final year at school, when they should actually be knuckling down. And to those super socialite kids, who view school as just a mere inconvenience on their drive to popularity and partying, we admire your hutzpah! It seems many in this generation are party PR enhanced – they know how to connect. One day these kids will have big jobs in IT, run companies or be Prime Minister.

## SCHOOLIES

Every year in November the big Australian holiday towns are overrun by 'schoolies' (school leavers, crazed with the excitement of fun, freedom and liberation). Some places have organised fun, where packs of kids from all over the country jam into cheap high-rise hotel rooms and head out to mass parties. These special school leavers centres can be extremely well organised and well policed: kids need wristbands to drink alcohol and can still have a pass to dance events if they are under 18. There might even be volunteer helpers, such as the 'Red Frogs' who check on the drinking, a 24-hour helpline for parents and students, and comprehensive security arrangements in approved properties. It can be tough if your teen isn't yet 18 and all their friends are – you don't want them at separate parties, or having to sit outside clubs and wait for the group. But there's always fake ID. Don't gasp: didn't you have one? Depending on how good it is, know it will work better in some places than others. The more popular holiday places will fleece them big time and they will pay through the nose. And they need to be aware the rules of occupancy are strictly policed: if a group of kids in a three-bedroom flat have a friend over during the day and there's a random inspection, they can be turfed out onto the street.

Other places won't be as well patrolled, and might still have opportunist 'toolies' (sleazebags who go to prey on young girls) and less supervision.

Schoolies is scary for parents. The biggest dangers are alcohol and balconies. But you have to trust your teen because they are now either an adult or very close to it. Don't panic if they don't answer the phone, but try to get them to check in once a day.

The latest trend is for parents to become 'poolies' and go with their child to schoolies. They often stay at a nearby resort to be close. Yes, it's helicopter parenting, but if you don't mind the cost and your kid is ok with it, well, lucky you. Or you could have your own holiday. An OOH week . . . an 'off our hands' holiday of relief and celebration that your teen has finished school. You've done a lot of emotional work in those final years of school, and we get it. Don't crash their holiday – have your own. But know that your teen might think you are stealing their thang.

S is also for . . . Stomping, Sighing, Sarcasm, Self-conscious, Sullen . . . but, stop it: that's their job!

T is for ... torpor.

# T

## IS FOR . . .

TORPOR, TALKING BACK,
TESTES, TIME, TEACHERS,
TECHNOLOGY SKILLS,
TRANS, TRUST

## TORPOR

Teen torpor is just wonderful to watch. That lanky body unfolds like a decaying flower then listlessly drags its legs to slump sloth-like at the table. Some teens enter the room like a parched explorer crossing the desert and close to death. Dragging their feet to the fridge, they might then find the sudden burst of energy needed to throw themselves on the couch, only to fall back into a deep torpor. They've been tired all day and awake half the night and they just can't deal. (*See also L is for Lazy and lethargic.*)

## TALKING BACK

Your word comes from on high and should be taken as gospel. How dare they question it, argue with it or respond to your genius with 'That's not fair' or 'I don't have to listen to you', or 'What would you know?' or worse? Thanks to plenty of training and practice we can put up with any of the above but we won't tolerate rude put-downs, swearing that's worse than ours or character assassination. Genuinely challenging you on issues in areas they feel you know nothing about is not talking back. Respectful questioning and critical thinking is not talking back. But cruel, disrespect and disorder is talking back. We try to stay calm, issue a warning and follow through on what that warning said. However, we usually fail and yell 'Because I said so!'. It's ideal to delay these testy conversations until you are all calm and rational. Like when they're 20.

# TESTES . . .

. . . must be touched regularly or they might fall off. Some teen boys can learn to do everything one-handed between the ages of 14 and 18. It's a gift.

# TIME

Teen time is different to adult time. They live in a warp, which means there's a time differential equation just waiting to be discovered. We'd award a Nobel Prize to the mathematician who works out just how long a 15-year-old means by 'in a minute' when asked to empty the dishwasher. Teen time is relative; a yell of 'coming' will mean 'now' if it refers to coming to dinner, but for the dishwasher emptying, a minute usually means hours. If it's in response to 'Please take the rubbish out,' it could mean weeks. If it's after you've yelled 'Clean your room, for God's sake,' it could mean months. The formula needs to incorporate the fact that, for you, these requests are reasonable, but for an adolescent they're an outrageous assault on their teen rights. Don't you know there's a meme that must be laughed at, a group chat that must be joined, a TikTok that must be filmed and an Insta story that must be love-hearted first? They just don't have time for your boring, banal bull.

Time usually moves more slowly for a teen. A maths lesson can feel like a day, a school week like a month, and a term like most of their natural life. Yet the holidays go fast. Until they are about 13, next year is too far into the future for many to even consider. Further long-term planning doesn't fit into a teen's sense of time at all. Lecturing about long-term harm from nicotine just doesn't compute to a child who feels next year is eons away. Fifty years on is simply inconceivable.

Time management is the hardest thing to learn at high school. That assignment due in a week is zillions of years away – there is no point in starting soon. Help them draw up charts for what they've got to do, or have the term's assignment dates stuck on the fridge if they struggle.

Then there's your time. It's precious. Give it to them. Spend time with them every week investing in a shared experience they enjoy, even if it's just a hamburger, a walk, a TV show; something that tells them they matter, that you are on their side. In our experience, the teen needs as much of your time as when they were a toddler. They need to know you are there for them and, while they might seem independent, they actually do want you to be present and connected. You all need time to vent, time to laugh, time to veg, time to work out what is going on with them (and what they might need to apologise for) and time together. Because soon they won't have much time for you at all.

# TEACHERS . . .

. . . should be worshipped. They have a hell of a job. Think about it: they have to teach huge groups of teens, while you can hardly deal with one. No wonder they are 'horrible/boring/mean/hopeless/suck/too fast/too slow/waffle off topic/stick too much to the book/explain too much/don't explain enough/won't reveal what's in the exam'. Sometimes your child will love a teacher, call them a 'legend' or feel inspired by their excitement for their subject.

Give that teacher a bottle of something and your never-ending devotion.

## TECHNOLOGY SKILLS

Their tech skills will always be better than yours. It's likely they can get around your YouTube and porn-blockers, and that your Net Nanny is mere sport to them. They might be able to impersonate you online, turn off the tracker you've got on their phone, and book a flight to Iceland on your iPad. So use them to fix their grandparents' technology gremlins and go for honesty and openness.

## TRANS

If your child comes out as queer or gender fluid and starts wearing the clothes of the opposite sex, then know that later they might come out as trans. Or, they might not. Trans teens seem to be becoming more common but this doesn't make it any less of a shock when it happens in your family. Some kids gave clues when they were younger, always preferring the clothes and toys of the opposite sex, but for some it comes completely out of the blue.

Mum! There's something wrong with this mirror!

Trans means transgender. It means your teen wants to have a gender identity or expression that is different from their assigned sex.

Or it could mean your teen wants to be non-binary or non-defined in terms of identity, or even sees themselves as a third gender.

If your child tells you they are trans, don't freak out. Ask them what they mean by that but be aware they may not know exactly what they want yet. Stay calm. Don't panic. It's not about you; it's about them. Be open and keep your worries and stress to yourself. Don't dismiss it as a phase, even if you think it is; take them seriously. Tell them you love them and you will help them work out what they need to be happy in their skin. Then, if you need to, go and scream with shock into your pillow.

If your child is trans, it might mean they want to dress differently, change their hair style, and change their name, or the pronoun they go by (he or she). They might even want that pronoun to be 'they', which enrages some but is a small word to cause so much angst. It might mean they want to change their hormones with medication or even, ultimately, have surgery.

Remember, your child is still your child. The same child you love and rocked and fed and played with and patted to sleep. They just now have a different path in life to the one you expected. There are many things for them to deal with – the physical, the emotional, the psychological, the social. They might be frightened, depressed, confused and very worried. So might you. Be their sanctuary, then get support for them and for yourself. Take your teen to your GP, who will probably refer you to a psychiatrist.

Gender dysphoria is a diagnosis that can only be made by experts, but it's likely your teen could be a lay expert already. They can get a lot of information online, so many are already familiar with the language of gender fluidity and trans. If your kid comes home and tells you about a trans kid at school, they'll most likely be pretty comfortable with it. Some schools are enormously supportive of such students, some are not. If your teen is at a single-sex school or a religious one it can be more difficult. Make an appointment with the principal and the school counsellor and find out their approach. Some Catholic schools are surprisingly supportive, but it depends on the school and the leadership. Moving schools is a big issue; the professionals will help you and your teen make the best decisions.

They will also help you make the other decisions that loom large, such as how to tell other family members, confused grandparents and family friends. Trans is not about sex, but if they have a partner or sexual orientation and keep it, they might go from heterosexual to queer. Yes, it's huge, it's confusing and bewildering and a whole new world will open up to you. Do your research and turn towards facts not fear.

## TRUST

You can't trust your teen completely. Sorry. Some can be trusted more than others, some not at all. Research from the University of Wisconsin called 'Other Kids Drink, But Not My Kid', found that although *all* the high school students in the study drank, only one-third of their parents knew. Parents felt that 'teens in general' drank, and that many of their own child's friends drank, but not *their child*. Which made us shudder, because we are a bit like that. But that's because *our* kids don't drink and never will.

Parents are in a bit of a catch 22 in terms of trust. Teens want and need to feel trusted. And, generally, if they feel trusted they will be more inspired to behave in ways that live up to and keep that trust. And teens who feel deeply distrusted will be resentful and become estranged from you. They won't bother telling you anything and will have little incentive to behave properly. Give trust where it's deserved and in increasing doses, but don't blindly trust or you might miss warning signs and the opportunity to give good advice.

It's vital to try to get your kids to trust you. You want to be the parent they tell when there is drinking, drug-taking and misbehaviour going on. But don't be the parent who tells other parents this trusted information. You have to earn your teen's trust. Tell them you won't blab – unless lives are in danger and then all bets are off.

U is for... university

# U

## IS FOR . . .

UNIVERSITY,
UNFAIR,
UNDERSTAND

## UNIVERSITY

This is a worthy goal but it's not for everyone. Some teens will be keen to get a trade or head straight into the workforce.

Tertiary education has changed a lot in recent years. Universities are now big business and are increasingly professionalised, marketed and slick. If your child is keen to attend university, support their goal but remind them there are more ways to get in than by their final grades alone.

Starting university can be overwhelming after all the care, consideration and attention they've had at school. It's a leap as big as starting high school again and teens who have enjoyed the most cloistered of school environments often struggle more. Some find it overwhelming and need to develop more skills of independence, such as self-discipline, seeking out information and thinking critically. The critical thinking is especially hard for those who have been the most spoon-fed for the final leaving exams. It can seem like a giant leap from the small school pond.

But it's their leap, not yours. University lecturers are reportedly horrified by the increasing interference by parents into the lives of new students. Parents of young adults are now emailing tutors and demanding better marks for their baby. One university law school has even introduced a parent–teacher night. Let it go, parents. Let it go.

If they are not ready for university, a trade, or other study, they might take a gap year, or two. This can help them grow up a bit, travel, work, learn some living skills and feel more independent and self-sufficient. It can also help teens work out what they actually want to study and why. Having a crappy job for a while really focuses the mind on what they *don't* want to do. Lecturers report that they can always spot the kids who've had a gap year – they are tougher, less teary and have less fear of failure. There's even research showing that those who take a gap year actually achieve better academic results at university. The final year of school can be exhausting and take away all the pleasure of learning. They might need time to reclaim that.

Encourage your teen to embrace the gap year as a time of freedom, development and learning. Not for smoking bongs in bed. Casual jobs are not what they used to be, but there's still work to be found in supermarkets, cafes, bars, tutoring or dog-walking. Many kids are now signing up for organised breaks to experience life volunteering for charities in South America, Africa and Asia. Explore the pros and cons with your teen and encourage them to think about the ethics. What will they be doing and what good is that doing? Are they taking a job from a local, or providing a vital service? What motivation do they have? Cultural exchange or cute kids for their Instagram page?

Beware of 'voluntourism' and the western saviour complex – building a bad wall in an orphanage might take away the jobs of local builders, who will do it better anyway. It's complicated and they must do their research.

Other opportunities include supervising rich English public school kids for a little cash and a lot of fun holidays. Or the American summer camp system that has been going for decades. They won't get paid much, but it's safe and they can reenact all those American movies they've watched over the years.

As to what they study and whether university is worth it, well that's an entirely different question. Universities are grappling with the changing nature of work, technology and society. Critical thinking is now increasingly important, as well as adaptability. This generation will need to know how to concentrate enough to do deep work. Focus is a key skill and they will need to be life-long learners.

Universities are becoming more expensive and your child will come out with a debt. There's also a growing trend for students to study overseas for a semester or year – lucky things – if you can afford it. Postgraduate study is also becoming increasingly common; one degree is often not enough anymore. So, don't plan your retirement. It may never happen.

And if you're going with them to open days and information talks, you might just find you love the idea of going to university yourself. Then you could yell across the lecture theatre 'Hey, darling boy, come have a drink with me in the bar' and be one of those mature-aged students who annoyed us all by starting their assignments immediately, always doing the reading, and getting far better marks than the rest of the year.

## UNFAIR

Life is so unfair for a teen. The most popular girl gets the main part in the play they wanted, they aren't picked for the athletics team, they've got the only crap art teacher in the whole school, clothes don't fit their body properly, they didn't get a car for their sixteenth birthday . . . Life can seem insurmountably unfair and cruel.

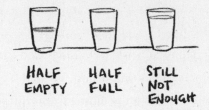

HALF EMPTY    HALF FULL    STILL NOT ENOUGH

If your kid is feeling hardly done by, perhaps you need to turn their gaze and zoom their perspective out a little to consider those who haven't got it as good. They might also need to take a soft reality check and manage their expectations.

But sometimes they are right. Life is unfair and you have to tell them so. Realising this is part of growing up, and you need to know that it's not your job to make everything all right for them.

While they can become better than they are, the dream-it-and-you-can-be-it cliché is hard to believe in. Be aware of the toxic positivity and empty inspiration of cliche culture. Disney dreams don't last. Reality will kick in during the teenage years. Encourage them to strive for what they want, but be prepared for things not to work out like the dream.

## UNDERSTAND

You don't. You can't.

And 'stop trying to relate, it's really annoying'.

V is for ... vegan

# V

## IS FOR . . .

VEGAN,
VAPING,
VERNACULAR

## VEGAN

This is becoming increasingly common for teens. We know a few who have been vegan for hours (until their first taste of soy milk), weeks (until the first vegie sausage) and years (still going). We also know some stridently defiant carnivores who would wear and eat Lady Gaga's meat dress if given half the chance.

Vegans are kids with a conscience. They understand that eating meat causes animals to be born to die and, while we won't get into the debate here, you should respect them for taking a personal, political and inter-species stance. Don't tease them with steak, but do talk about nutrition. Seek out proper research, not the rubbish they might read. Consider regular blood tests to check their iron levels (this tests both iron and commitment: we know one 13-year-old who was vegan until the doctor's appointment was booked). If their iron levels are low, they will need supplements.

Get them to help with the cooking and go meat-free yourself for a few days a week – it will reduce extra washing-up and your carbon imprint and, quite possibly, improve your health. One teen we know went macrobiotic and her parents said 'fine, but you cook'. Saucepans stuck with brown rice, mushy vegetables and tempeh littered the kitchen for weeks until the heroic health kick tuckered out due to laziness.

## VAPING

Unfortunately, it's become cool for some teens to vape, just like smoking was in your day. There are online videos of good-looking kids doing amazing tricks to funky music that your teen will probably have seen. This means vaping is on the up, up, up and you need to be on the lookout for it. The American Centre for Disease Control and Prevention estimates 3.6 million adolescents were vaping in 2018. The e-cigarette companies are deliberately targeting teens with e-liquid flavourings such as cinnamon roll, cotton candy, melon, pineapple, chocolate, coconut and cherry. Nice work, people.

This means that if your teen is vaping, they might not smell like the ciggies you recognise; they could smell like cheap perfume. What's more, their e-cigarette can look like a pen, a computer memory stick or flash drive, a car key fob, even an asthma inhaler. Vaping involves inhaling 'e-juice' that has been heated with a battery-powered coil. The juice could contain nicotine, even if it's not meant to, or THC (the active ingredient in marijuana, which may be what they're after). Vaping is marketed as safe and cool, but, of course, it's not.

They won't know what they are vaping. A study published in *The Medical Journal of Australia* analysed the liquid in 'nicotine-free' e-cigarettes sold online and over-the-counter and found 60 per cent of them contained nicotine, a highly addictive stimulant. All held traces of a toxic chemical (2-chlorophenol), commonly used in insecticides, herbicides and disinfectants. Ingredients often used in soaps, detergents and solvents were also found. Early toxicology tests are showing a number of e-liquid flavouring chemicals caused high levels of cell stress. Deaths due to e-cigarettes have been identified and verified; they are believed to be particularly linked with the vaping of cannabis oil, which then solidifies on the lungs. Of course, your teen probably feels immune and untouchable to what hurts ordinary mortals. So warn them about the oils and the latest information ... and then tell them they could be sucking on poo. The study also found by-products of animal or human bodily functions in e-liquids. Don't suck on poo: it ain't cool, kids.

Some experts point out that vaping has reduced smoking in teens and that's a good thing. And it's definitely helped some adults stop smoking near their teens, which is also good. But it's best they never start either.

Some older teens take up old-fashioned smoking as they start university or join the workforce, which is disappointing and weird and expensive. Perhaps it's an expression of nihilism that hopefully won't last.

## VERNACULAR

We love the teen vernacular. There's an entirely new language forming in this generation and we are 'down for it'. You might overhear sentences such as 'sliding into my DMs', 'the fat leg was friend-zoning me, which triggered me big time', 'better than ghosting but, seriously, it was whack'. 'OMG fight me cos I'm the

OG stan' and 'stop casting shade'. We also like 'Don't dog the boys', 'Spill the T' (tell us the gossip), yeet, Gucci (good), li, soshe (social media), salty, frothing, legit, lush, flex, chime, sack (bad), eshay, I've got beef (I've got an issue with you), trek (it's too far) fat trek (it's way too far), search it up

(Google it) and totes awkie. And, when a hot guy walks past, 'OMG I'm literally pregnant'.

But do be aware: now we've written this vernacular down on paper, it means it's known by adults and therefore long extinct. If you try any of these phrases on your teen you will get the sort of withering glance that could fell a T-Rex. Don't be a Desmond.

Teens trade in a constantly shifting and evolving visual culture of memes and half-remembered vines. It's what gives them membership of the teen tribe. You can't keep up. Best not to try.

W is for... woke

# W

## IS FOR . . .

WOKE, WISDOM TEETH,
WARS OVER HOMEWORK,
WORRY, WATCH,
WET DREAMS,
WHATEVER

# WOKE

The teens of today analyse fiction not just for its subtext, themes and meaning, but also for its heteronormative characters. Many are furious at their one-time idol JK Rowling for suggesting Dumbledore is gay (queerbaiting) and some even accuse her of being a TERF (trans exclusionary radical feminist). Their intersectional focus on feminism and their genderqueer analysis of the queue at Woolies will amaze you.

They are a very aware generation; aware of race, gender norms and prevailing sexism. They might not know who Harvey Weinstein is, but they know we need a great lesbian feminist Bond ASAP.

Woke is not an insult, but it can lead to intergenerational confusion. At times you might feel you are walking on eggshells during conversations about popular culture and you could be pulled up by your teen for calling your poodle pathetic. 'He's gender fluid, Mum. Deal with it. It's his right to prance, and get that blue collar off him: it's gender stereotyping him as male when you cut his balls off years ago anyway.'

Of course, not all teens are woke. And some teens are post-woke. They are reacting to their earlier wokeness, or the wokeness around them, with irony, a fond sense of self-mockery or a huge dose of Chris Lilley. This means they can say things that sound sexist, racist and gender stereotypical, but get away with it because it's ironic. Don't ever try this yourself. You will get it wrong and be offensive.

# WISDOM TEETH

The getting of wisdom teeth can really wreck a 10,000 dollar set of beautiful teeth that you've just finished paying for after braces and expanders. Talk to their dentist or orthodontist. If they need them extracting, it will hurt and they will look like a chipmunk and need ice cream, soup and love.

## WARS OVER HOMEWORK

The dreaded homework steps up in high school and can be a tough one to negotiate and deal with. Some parents want all homework done before allowing screen time or gaming, while some teens really need to knock off for the day and have a break first. Some can work alone in their room without being distracted by their phone, social media and Facetiming an object of affection, while others need support and constant harassment at the kitchen table. Some schools give so much homework it's ridiculous, others set long-term assignments and some seem to do very little. Try to help your teen plan ahead so it's not done all at the last minute the night before it's due through a veil of tears and the gnashing of your teeth. Planning is important and can be learned (imagine an emoji of laughing tears here). Do declare truce times such as Friday nights and holidays and hope this particular war will be over by their final year of high school.

## WORRY

You will. All the time. But try to worry about the important things: not so much their marks, sporting prowess and disgusting  habits, but rather their survival, developing competence, resilience and reasonable happiness. If you have huge worries about your teen, and we know many parents do, we feel very deeply for you. It can be terrifying when they are deeply troubled or in deep trouble. You just want to take their turmoil and pain and make it yours, so that you can all breathe again. But, of course, you can't and that's excruciating. Make sure you are getting all the help you need so you can help them. Find a time you can set worry aside every day if you must, but nothing reduces worry like action. If niggles persist about your teen, seek information and help.

## WATCH

Watch with them. You already know our favourite is *Buffy the Vampire Slayer* but many of them also enjoy retro stuff like *Friends* (but do tell them girl-kissing is not about male titillation, despite how funny Chandler and Joey are), or *The Office* and *Stranger Things* and *Brooklyn Nine-Nine*. Watch whatever they are watching, even if it's tacky and hideous. You can use it as a learning experience and a topic to get them talking. You might even find it fun.

## WET DREAMS

In polite company, these are called 'nocturnal emissions'. They can happen during puberty as the teen boy makes more testosterone. Warn your teen in a matter-of-fact way that he might have a sexy dream and wake up in a bit of a wet spot after ejaculating. It's nothing to worry about, nor feel guilty about. Teach him to change his sheets and put his PJs in the wash to avoid embarrassment if he feels upset about it. Girls have wet dreams too and might wake up aroused or with extra vaginal secretions.

Boys can also get random erections, 'boners', 'hard-ons' or 'stiffs' during daylight hours and, of course, these will occur at the most inconvenient and embarrassing times. They will hear all about them in the playground but pre-warning is always helpful. Long shirts are fabulous for the teen years so, luckily, baggy clothing is in. Your boy can try shifting positions, adjusting his clothes, relaxing, thinking of other things such as maths tests or assignments to bring it down. Tell him how common they are and that he will gain control as he grows older.

## WHATEVER
You've heard it a lot – you don't need to hear it from us.

X is for... X-rated

# X

# IS FOR . . .

## X-RATED

You might have come across a *Playboy* magazine or a grainy porn VHS or even a racy *National Geographic* at 15 and it was probably titillating and funny. But your teen or tween could have been sweetly searching the internet for piano-playing pussy cats and seen something they can never un-see. Or they might be sitting in double Geography, minding their own business, when the child next to them airdrops a video of double penetration. They could be on a kids' gaming site that has been hijacked and see x-rated porn. We've heard stories of a 13-year-old at camp watching porn in the cabin and then suggesting to the others bunking in with her that they 'all get down to sex'. We've heard about kids perusing internet porn during Maths class, which is just not the way Pythagoras imagined his work would be investigated, we're sure.

It's shocking and awful and they are just not ready for it. Indeed, seeing porn might freak them out and scar them – one Australian study found they can be haunted by flashbacks for a long time. Of course, they can also find porn fascinating and exciting. They might feel all those things at once.

This is an awful subject to broach with them, but talk you must. Schools talk to them about it a bit, but you have to do it too. Tell your teen that if an adult is showing them porn, they are, most likely, being groomed for abuse. If they tell you this is happening, ring the local police station. Teens also need to know that if they are sent pictures of underage sex acts it is illegal sharing and should be deleted immediately. Sixty-nine (ha ha) per cent of parents believe it's essential to educate their kids about pornography and three-quarters see themselves as responsible for providing this education in the home. Yet less than half of us report actually speaking to our children about pornography. We get why it's hard. God, it's hard. We'll stop saying hard now.

They need to know about porn and what it really is. That porn is not real life; that it's unreal, exaggerated, sometimes violent, exploitative, disrespectful and not safe. Tell them the sex might not be the sex they want. Tell your son he shouldn't assume that girls or boys want to have anal sex and other sex acts that paid porn actors pretend to want. Talk to your daughter about her real desire versus performative porn desire. Tell them they don't need to pretend to enjoy sex acts that actually hurt or that they are uncomfortable with. Tell them that if they expect sexual partners to be porn stars they are bullies. Sex should be fun, playful, enjoyable – porn can take away those elements.

Acknowledge that for many teens porn is now their sex education, and that's not necessarily a good thing when it comes to learning about real versus fake pleasure, consent and respect. (*See C is for consent.*) Talk to them about trust and emotional closeness and how that can enhance sexual pleasure. There's real concern expressed by parents about how porn is impacting young relationships, and so there should be.

The most effective strategy is to have conversations about the types of situations they might face and explore the ways they could respond. These scenarios might include friends pressurising them to watch porn. Should they just ignore it, tell their friend they don't want to watch it, or find some way to remove themselves from the situation? Or should they watch it? They won't be the first or the last.

Also talk to them about body types and images in porn. How not all men have giant penises and that the female participants can be surgically enhanced and falsified. Yes, we know there's realistic home-made porn, but they might not see that.

These conversations are super-confronting and awkward and we're not claiming that we've had them adequately ourselves. We are hypocrites. We found the government website for e-safety has good advice and age-appropriate tips about starting the chat and how to talk about sex and pornography without hectoring. It's important to not be too aggressive and antagonistic – they won't tell you things if you ban and damn. If you are cooking and are asked a question about porn or sex, keep cutting up those cucumbers and stay calm. Moderate your voice. Don't panic. Stay shoulder to shoulder and avoid eye contact.

Oh, and if you think your child doesn't know what porn is, you need to wake up. One friend claimed to be mystified at how much time her 16-year-old son was spending on the loo with his phone. We didn't have the heart to tell her he was probably watching porn. After all, he might have been constipated. If this situation sounds familiar, buy prunes or talk porn. Please.

Y is for ... yelling

# Y

## IS FOR . . .

YELLING,
YES,
YAWN,
YEAR GROUP

## YELLING

We once heard a teenage girl yelling blue murder at her mother in front of their house: 'I hate you! What the hell would you know?'

We couldn't make out the mother's response as it came as a low rumble.

The teen responded with a howl: 'You have no idea! You are so dumb!'

Mumble calm rumble.

'I'm leaving, you cow!' was followed by a screech of tyres and a P plate falling off in the driveway.

We were in awe of this mother. She had stayed calm and serene and quiet in the face of the yelling. We peeked through the fence to observe this superwoman of serenity. She was standing there in the dust of the tyres, tears rolling down her face, her fists and teeth clenched tight.

'Bitch,' she spat out. Then she turned on her heel and headed inside.

A mother monk. Our idol.

## YES

Sometimes having a teen is just a world of no.

'Can I have a Fender Stratocaster guitar?'

'No.'

'Can I go to this sleepover party where there aren't any parents?'

'No.'

'Can I borrow your car and drive all my friends to that sleepover party?'

'No.'

If you feel like you're always saying no, then try to say yes to some easy things such as 'Can I have cheese with that?' or 'Can I wear this frightful outfit?' Pick your battles.

## YAWN

You will see a lot of yawns. Morning, noon and night. Teens can be tired a lot. *(See Z is for Zzzzzz.)* The yawn seems rude, but it can be a good time to check their tonsils aren't swollen and their dental hygiene is passable. It is catching though, so too many teen yawns could send you into a torpor or for an afternoon nap.

## YEAR GROUP

Sometimes your kid will be in a year group that's supportive and wonderful, fun and energetic. Sometimes they will be in a year group of shockers. It's a weird magic. But, of course, in most years there will be a mix of kids and not always a dominant culture. If it is a toxic team, sometimes a couple of ringleaders leave and it settles. We try not to let our teens buy into the idea of bad versus good school years, but we know it can actually happen.

If it's affecting your teen, you might need to change schools, but this is often easier said than done. Finding another school that is convenient and has a spot, or trying to afford a private school, is often beyond tricky or beyond your means. If you can't move schools, perhaps help your teen find friends outside their year and outside their school instead. They could join a local drama group, sports team, church youth group or Scouts. This will expand their horizons in life beyond their small school pool.

Things will often calm down within their year as they all get older and wiser. Sometimes even the teens who hated their year group spend the last year of school hugging and making peace with the people they loathed.

Z is for... ZZZZZZ

# Z

# IS FOR . . .

ZZZZZZ,
ZITS

# ZZZZZ

Our babies never slept. One dozed in 45-minute blocks, another in tantalising 20-minute catnaps. We read every sleep book, sought endless advice and went off to baby sleep camp. They failed. We patted, wrapped, rocked, crooned, cocooned, carried, drove, dummied, did everything. Now they're teens and most days we can't wake them up.

Sound familiar?

Teens' body clocks change around the age of 15. Their biorhythms switch so suddenly that they go from 6am starts to not being able to get to sleep at night and impossible to wake up in the morning. Their bodies are telling them to stay out and roam under the full moon, not get up for basketball practice and early class. They are fighting society on this. Some schools have moved timetables to start classes later, but most refuse. This means you have a sleepy, cranky adolescent you might have to yank out of bed in the morning with a cup of tea, a cold flannel or a blast of bad music. It also means they can spend the morning and early afternoon feeling like zombies.

But that is not the only reason this generation of teens is not getting enough sleep. The American Academy of Pediatrics recommends that teens aged between 13 and 18 get 8–10 hours of sleep on a regular basis to promote optimal health. Your teen might need more or they might need less, but most are finding that hard. It's not just the homework that's keeping them up. Their brain, just like yours, is being kept awake by a mobile device. In just the same way you might have read *Puberty Blues* with a torch under the blankets, many teens today are sleeping with their phone in their bed. More than a third are waking up to check their social media or logging back on after pretending to be asleep – that artful soft snore as you kiss them goodnight is the ultimate giveaway. Then, when they first wake in the morning, they roll over and check their social media before they are even fully conscious.

Just like when they were babies, teens need a consistent routine before bye-byes. We suggest reading and snuggling with a warm wheat bag and shutting down all screens an hour before they try to nod off. If they can't control themselves, remove their computer, phone or iPad from the room to take away all temptation. They will scream that they need the alarm on the phone, but you can introduce them to the old-fashioned concept of an alarm clock. It's retro, baby! (But yes, it's also a pain in the butt as we just can't cope with analogue anymore.) Or you could demand you keep the phone in your room and you wake them up in the morning.

May we suggest shutting down the modem for the entire house at 9.30pm, or using flight mode to block out the tempting stuff on the phone. You should do it too: you'll sleep better. We admit massive hypocrisy on this front – we always have our phones on until lights out.

Weekends are for catching up. But trying to turn their body clock around within 72 hours is just asking for trouble. If you let your teen sleep until lunchtime on Saturday or Sunday, then Monday becomes a fresh new hell. They could feel they are in a state of permanent jet lag. Of course, going in and waking them up before noon on a Sunday is also dangerous. We suggest sending in the dog or a younger sibling to lick their face, but sometimes nothing works except the shake and yell that means they will hate you just that little bit more.

It was once thought you couldn't 'bank sleep' to use later but some recent research suggests you can. Sleep experts suggest that getting up two hours later at the weekend is doable, but warn if you let them go too long they stuff up their sleep cycle. So wake them around 9 and enjoy that extra morning time to walk around nude or have your daggy old music on in a tidy house.

Holidays are for Zzzzz. Let them lie in that Land of Nod for as long as they like, unless it's giving them bedsores. Holidays should be holidays. Returning to school after the long, sleepy, late-night summer break is particularly gruesome. We start getting up earlier and going to bed an hour earlier every day for the week beforehand, but it's still never pretty. A rumpled zonked-out teen is either adorable or infuriating, but rarely anything in between. As neither of us is a morning person, we relate.

## ZITS

Zits suck. Just when your teen starts to really care about their appearance, up they pop. It can physically hurt to look at that beautiful face so red and swollen with pus. So imagine what it's like for them! Pimples can come and go but sometimes they can last for years. They can be annoying or deeply distressing, depending on their severity.

Almost all teens will get zits or acne and if you or their other parent had bad skin then they are more prone. It's all thanks to hormones called androgens, which increase the production of oily sebum that clogs their pores.

Try to convince your teen not to over-wash their face or they might irritate the skin into producing even more oil. Gentle cleaning twice a day with soap-free products and lots of water is good. Over-the-counter benzoyl peroxide washes are very good for mild cases. Teen girls love face masks – check they are not using masks that exacerbate rather than help. Popping or squeezing zits is bad, no matter how joyful for you or their mates. We were always told that a healthy diet with lots of greens, giving up chocolate, getting plenty of sleep and drinking a lot of water would cure zits but, while these can help and are all great for general health, they can't turn off the hormones. Stress won't cause zits but it can make them worse.

Get help if your teen's self-esteem plummets or they are getting teased. It's all very well for you to say looks aren't everything, but you don't live in their world. Most cases of zits, blackheads and whiteheads will clear up with age and time and care, but if your teen is developing big pustules and cysts then chances are they'll be in pain and getting distressed. Take them to the GP who can prescribe effective antibiotics, or some girls might go on the pill to help balance their hormones. For severe acne there is isotretinoin (Accutane), but this must be prescribed by experts and can have some dangerous side effects.

It irks us that while having teens we've been so run down and tired that we've got zits ourselves. We did hope that between pimples and wrinkles there could have been some years of beauty. Nope.

# THANK YOU AND GOODBYE

And then, suddenly, it's all over. Your child grows up, becomes an adult and, just when you realise you want to spend a lot more time with them, they're gone.

Congratulations and commiserations. We hope we've helped a little, made you feel less alone, or at the very least made you laugh. The worst is over, but now you'll miss them like hell.

Perhaps now you can go and live in a yurt in Mongolia, or have time to take up sky-diving or nude banjo-playing. However, it's most likely you'll have to keep working to support them, because your job is not done. They are a boomerang generation. They will come back, perhaps with a partner or maybe, one day, a baby. Gulp. They can't afford a house until you die, so you'll have to get used to living with them for a while longer, and in a different way.

Please suggest this book to other parents who are pulling their hair out in traffic with an L-plated driver, buying a roast chook every day as an afternoon teen 'snack', or spending hours energetically arguing about nothing. Give it to friends on their child's thirteenth birthday. Why should kids get all the presents after all?

You're the one who deserves the gifts, medals and full ticker-tape parade.

Thank you for raising the next generation. They are utterly brilliant, wonderful and gorgeous. And a lot of that is thanks to you. You are da bomb.

# ACKNOWLEDGEMENTS

Our endless love and eternal gratitude to our teens and post-teen children: Sophie, Felix, Georgie and Gus. You are awesome and we adore you. Thanks to their wonderful fathers, Giles and Jonathan, for their steadfast support.

Thanks to Jocelyn Brewer for her educated and professional feedback on the work.

Huge thanks to our fabulous editor, Jane Price, our incredible ideas woman, publisher Jane Morrow, and boss lady Lou Johnson, for their enthusiasm, understanding, guidance and brilliance.

To the teens of today: we love you. Go grab your future.